# BALLADS OF BOOKS

## LECTOR HOUSE PUBLIC DOMAIN WORKS

This book is a result of an effort made by Lector House towards making a contribution to the preservation and repair of original classic literature. The original text is in the public domain in the United States of America, and possibly other countries depending upon their specific copyright laws.

In an attempt to preserve, improve and recreate the original content, certain conventional norms with regard to typographical mistakes, hyphenations, punctuations and/or other related subject matters, have been corrected upon our consideration. However, few such imperfections might not have been rectified as they were inherited and preserved from the original content to maintain the authenticity and construct, relevant to the work. The work might contain a few prior copyright references as well as page references which have been retained, wherever considered relevant to the part of the construct. We believe that this work holds historical, cultural and/or intellectual importance in the literary works community, therefore despite the oddities, we accounted the work for print as a part of our continuing effort towards preservation of literary work and our contribution towards the development of the society as a whole, driven by our beliefs.

We are grateful to our readers for putting their faith in us and accepting our imperfections with regard to preservation of the historical content. We shall strive hard to meet up to the expectations to improve further to provide an enriching reading experience.

Though, we conduct extensive research in ascertaining the status of copyright before redeveloping a version of the content, in rare cases, a classic work might be incorrectly marked as not-in-copyright. In such cases, if you are the copyright holder, then kindly contact us or write to us, and we shall get back to you with an immediate course of action.

**HAPPY READING!**

# BALLADS OF BOOKS

## VARIOUS, BRANDER MATTHEWS

ISBN: 978-93-90198-88-7

Published: 1900

© 2020
LECTOR HOUSE LLP

**LECTOR HOUSE LLP**
E-MAIL: lectorpublishing@gmail.com

# BALLADS OF BOOKS

## CHOSEN BY

## BRANDER MATTHEWS

# TO
# FREDERICK LOCKER

## POET AND LOVER OF BOOKS

*Come and take a choice of all my library*

Titus Andronicus, iv. 1

# PREFATORY NOTE.

The poets have ever been lovers of books; indeed, one might ask how should a man be a poet who did not admire a treasure as precious and as beautiful as a book may be. With evident enjoyment, Keats describes

> A viol, bowstrings torn, cross-wise upon
> A glorious folio of Anacreon;

and it was a glorious folio of Beaumont and Fletcher which another English poet (whose most poetic work was done in prose) "dragged home late at night from Barker's in Covent Garden," and to pacify his conscience for the purchase of which he kept to his overworn suit of clothes for four or five weeks longer than he ought. Charles Lamb was a true bibliophile, in the earlier and more exact sense of the term; he loved his ragged volumes as he loved his fellow-men, and he was as intolerant of books that are not books as he was of men who were not manly. He conferred the dukedom of his library on Coleridge, who was no respecter of books, though he could not but enrich them with his marginal notes. Southey and Lord Houghton and Mr. Locker are English poets with libraries of their own, more orderly and far richer than the fortuitous congregation of printed atoms, a mere medley of unrelated tomes, which often masquerades as The Library in the mansions of the noble and the wealthy. Shelley said that he thought Southey had a secret in every one of his books which he was afraid the stranger might discover: but this was probably no more, and no other, than the secret of comfort, consolation, refreshment, and happiness to be found in any library by him who shall bring with him the golden key that unlocks its silent door.

Mr. Lowell has recently dwelt on the difference between literature and books: and, accepting this distinction, the editor desires to declare at once that as a whole this collection is devoted rather to books than to literature. The poems in the following pages celebrate the bric-a-brac of the one rather than the masterpieces of the other. The stanzas here garnered into one sheaf sing of books as books, of books valuable and valued for their perfection of type and page and printing,—for their beauty and for their rarity,—or for their association with some famous man

# PREFATORY NOTE.

or woman of the storied past

Two centuries and a half ago Drummond of Hawthornden prefixed to the 'Varieties' of his friend Persons a braggart distich:—

> This book a world is; here, if errors be,
> The like, nay worse, in the great world we see.

The present collection of varieties in verse has little or naught to do with the great world and its errors: it has to do chiefly, not to say wholly, with the world of the Bookmen—the little world of the Book-lover, the Bibliophile, the Bibliomaniac—a mad world, my masters, in which there are to be found not a few poets who cherish old wine and old wood, old friends and old books, and who believe that old books are the best of old friends.

> Books, books again, and books once more!
> These are our theme, which some miscall
> Mere madness, setting little store
> By copies either short or tall,
> But you, O slaves of shelf and stall!
> We rather write for you that hold
> Patched folios dear, and prize "the small
> Rare volume, black with burnished gold."

as Mr. Austin Dobson sang on the threshold of Mr. Lang's delightfully discursive little book about the 'Library.'

The editor has much pleasure in thanking the poets who have allowed him to reprint their poems in these pages; and he acknowledges a double debt of gratitude to the friends who have written poems expressly for this collection. Encouraged by their support, and remembering that he is not a contributor to his own pages, the editor ventures to conclude his harmless necessary catalogue of the things contained and not contained within these covers, by quoting Herrick's address to his Book:—

> Be bold, my Book, nor be abash'd, or fear,
> The cutting thumb-nail, or the brow severe;
> But by the muses swear, all here is good,
> If but well read, or ill read, understood.

BRANDER MATTHEWS.

New York, *November*, 1886.

# PROEM[1]

### BALLADE OF THE BOOKWORM.

*Deep in the Past I peer, and see*
*A Child upon the Nursery floor,*
*A Child with book, upon his knee,*
*Who asks, like Oliver, for more!*
*The number of his years is IV,*
*And yet in Letters hath he skill,*
*How deep he dives in Fairy-lore!*
*The Books I loved, I love them still!*

*One gift the Fairies gave me: (Three*
*They commonly bestowed of yore)*
*The Love of Books, the Golden Key*
*That opens the Enchanted Door;*
*Behind it BLUEBEARD lurks and o'er*
*And o'er doth JACK his Giants kill,*
*And there is all ALADDIN'S store,—*
*The Books I loved, I love them still!*

*Take all, but leave my Books to me!*
*These heavy creels of old we love*
*We fill not now, nor wander free,*
*Nor wear the heart that once we wore;*
*Not now each River seems to pour*
*His waters from the Muse's hill;*
*Though something's gone from stream and shore,*
*The Books I love, I love them still!*

### ENVOY!

---

[1] The poems thus marked were written or translated for the present collection.

# PROEM

*Fate, that art Queen by shore and sea,*
*We bow submissive to thy will,*
*Ah grant, by some benign decree,*
*The Books I loved — to love them still.*

A. Lang.

# CONTENTS

*Page*

- PREFATORY NOTE. . . . . . . . . . . . . . . . . . . . . . . . . . vi

## PROEM

- BALLADE OF THE BOOKWORM. . . . . . . . . . . . . . . . . . viii

## BALLADS OF BOOKS

- THE BABY IN THE LIBRARY. . . . . . . . . . . . . . . . . . . .1
- MY BOOKS. . . . . . . . . . . . . . . . . . . . . . . . . . . . . .2
- THE ART OF BOOK-KEEPING. . . . . . . . . . . . . . . . . . .2
- IN THE LIBRARY. . . . . . . . . . . . . . . . . . . . . . . . . .5
- MY SHAKSPERE. . . . . . . . . . . . . . . . . . . . . . . . . .6
- THE BOOKWORMS. . . . . . . . . . . . . . . . . . . . . . . . .7
- CATULLUS TO HIS BOOK. . . . . . . . . . . . . . . . . . . . .8
- OLD BOOKS ARE BEST. . . . . . . . . . . . . . . . . . . . . .8
- THE FORGOTTEN BOOKS. . . . . . . . . . . . . . . . . . . . .9
- AN INVOCATION IN A LIBRARY. . . . . . . . . . . . . . . . 10
- CONCERNING THE HONOR OF BOOKS. . . . . . . . . . . . 10
- LINES. . . . . . . . . . . . . . . . . . . . . . . . . . . . . . . 11
- MY BOOKS. . . . . . . . . . . . . . . . . . . . . . . . . . . . 11
- TO A MISSAL OF THE THIRTEENTH CENTURY. . . . . . . . 12
- THE BOOK-PLATE'S PETITION. . . . . . . . . . . . . . . . . 13

# CONTENTS

- OVER THE THRESHOLD OF MY LIBRARY.. . . . . . . . . . . . . . . . . . 14
- THE CHRYSALIS OF A BOOKWORM. . . . . . . . . . . . . . . . . . . . . 14
- EPIGRAM.. . . . . . . . . . . . . . . . . . . . . . . . . . . . . . . . . . . . . . . 15
- THE BIBLIOMANIA. . . . . . . . . . . . . . . . . . . . . . . . . . . . . . . . 15
- TRIOLET TO HER HUSBAND.. . . . . . . . . . . . . . . . . . . . . . . . . 20
- A NOOK AND A BOOK. . . . . . . . . . . . . . . . . . . . . . . . . . . . . . 20
- THE SULTAN OF MY BOOKS.. . . . . . . . . . . . . . . . . . . . . . . . . 21
- OUR BOOK-SHELVES. . . . . . . . . . . . . . . . . . . . . . . . . . . . . . 23
- TO HIS BOOK. . . . . . . . . . . . . . . . . . . . . . . . . . . . . . . . . . . . 24
- TO HIS BOOK. . . . . . . . . . . . . . . . . . . . . . . . . . . . . . . . . . . . 24
- TO HIS BOOKS. . . . . . . . . . . . . . . . . . . . . . . . . . . . . . . . . . . 24
- SONNET. . . . . . . . . . . . . . . . . . . . . . . . . . . . . . . . . . . . . . . . 25
- MY BOOKS.. . . . . . . . . . . . . . . . . . . . . . . . . . . . . . . . . . . . . 26
- TO MY BOOKSELLER. . . . . . . . . . . . . . . . . . . . . . . . . . . . . . 27
- TO SIR HENRY GOODYERE.. . . . . . . . . . . . . . . . . . . . . . . . . 27
- IN THE ALBUM OF LUCY BARTON.. . . . . . . . . . . . . . . . . . . . 28
- BALLADE OF THE BOOK-HUNTER.. . . . . . . . . . . . . . . . . . . . 28
- BALLADE OF TRUE WISDOM. . . . . . . . . . . . . . . . . . . . . . . . 29
- BALLADE OF THE BOOKMAN'S PARADISE.. . . . . . . . . . . . . . 30
- THE ROWFANT BOOKS. . . . . . . . . . . . . . . . . . . . . . . . . . . . . 31
- THE ROWFANT LIBRARY.. . . . . . . . . . . . . . . . . . . . . . . . . . . 31
- GHOSTS IN THE LIBRARY. . . . . . . . . . . . . . . . . . . . . . . . . . . 32
- THE BOOK BATTALION.. . . . . . . . . . . . . . . . . . . . . . . . . . . . 35
- ON THE FLY-LEAF OF A BOOK OF OLD PLAYS.. . . . . . . . . . . 36
- TOO MANY BOOKS. . . . . . . . . . . . . . . . . . . . . . . . . . . . . . . 36
- FROM THE FLY-LEAF OF THE ROWFANT MONTAIGNE (FLORIO, 1603).. . . . . . . . . . . . . . . . . . . . . . . . . . . . . . . . . . . . . . . . 37
- MY BOOKS.. . . . . . . . . . . . . . . . . . . . . . . . . . . . . . . . . . . . . 38

- THE SOULS OF BOOKS. . . . . . . . . . . . . . . . . . . . . . . . 38
- DE LIBRIS. . . . . . . . . . . . . . . . . . . . . . . . . . . . . . . . 41
- EX LIBRIS.. . . . . . . . . . . . . . . . . . . . . . . . . . . . . . . 42
- ON AN INSCRIPTION. . . . . . . . . . . . . . . . . . . . . . . 43
- TO MY BOOKS.. . . . . . . . . . . . . . . . . . . . . . . . . . . 44
- 'DESULTORY READING.' . . . . . . . . . . . . . . . . . . . 44
- THE BOOKWORM. . . . . . . . . . . . . . . . . . . . . . . . . 44
- AMONG MY BOOKS.. . . . . . . . . . . . . . . . . . . . . . . 47
- A RUINED LIBRARY. . . . . . . . . . . . . . . . . . . . . . . 47
- MY BOOKS.. . . . . . . . . . . . . . . . . . . . . . . . . . . . . 48
- TO MY BOOKS ON PARTING WITH THEM. . . . . . . 48
- AMONG MY BOOKS. . . . . . . . . . . . . . . . . . . . . . . 49
- THE LIBRARY. . . . . . . . . . . . . . . . . . . . . . . . . . . . 49
- IN THE LIBRARY. . . . . . . . . . . . . . . . . . . . . . . . . 50
- THE BOOK-HUNTER.. . . . . . . . . . . . . . . . . . . . . . 51
- THE LIBRARY. . . . . . . . . . . . . . . . . . . . . . . . . . . . 52
- PICTURE-BOOKS IN WINTER. . . . . . . . . . . . . . . . 53
- COMPANIONS. . . . . . . . . . . . . . . . . . . . . . . . . . . 53
- THE BOOK OF LIFE.. . . . . . . . . . . . . . . . . . . . . . 54
- ON CERTAIN BOOKS. . . . . . . . . . . . . . . . . . . . . . 55
- TO HIS BOOKS. . . . . . . . . . . . . . . . . . . . . . . . . . 56
- LITERATURE AND NATURE. . . . . . . . . . . . . . . . . 56
- THE LIBRARY. . . . . . . . . . . . . . . . . . . . . . . . . . . . 57
- THE COUNTRY SQUIRE.. . . . . . . . . . . . . . . . . . . 58
- OLD BOOKS. . . . . . . . . . . . . . . . . . . . . . . . . . . . 59

# APPENDIX

- THE LIBRARY. . . . . . . . . . . . . . . . . . . . . . . . . . . . 61

- A FINAL WORD..............................77

# BALLADS OF BOOKS

## THE BABY IN THE LIBRARY.

EDWARD D. ANDERSON. *From 'Wide-Awake' for May, 1885.*

Within these solemn, book-lined walls,
Did mortal ever see
A critic so unprejudiced,
So full of mirthful glee?

Just watch her at that lower shelf:
See, there she's thumped her nose
Against the place where Webster stands
In dignified repose.

Such heavy books she scorns; and she
Considers Vapereau,
And Beeton, too, though full of life,
Quite stupid, dull, and slow.

She wants to take a higher flight,
Aspiring little elf!
And on her mother's arm at length
She gains a higher shelf.

But, oh! What liberties she takes
With those grave, learnèd men;
Historians, and scientists,
And even "Rare old Ben!"

At times she takes a spiteful turn,
And pommels, with her fists,
De Quincey, Jeffrey, and Carlyle,
And other essayists.

And, when her wrath is fully roused,
And she's disposed for strife,
It almost looks as if she'd like
To take Macaulay's 'Life.'

Again, in sympathetic mood,
She gayly smiles at Gay,
And punches Punch, and frowns at Sterne

In quite a dreadful way.

In vain the Sermons shake their heads:
She does not care for these;
But catches, with intense delight,
At all the Tales she sees.

Where authors chance to meet her views,
Just praise they never lack;
To comfort and encourage them,
She pats them on the back.

## MY BOOKS.

Francis Bennoch. *From the 'Storm and Other Poems.' 1878.*

I love my books as drinkers love their wine;
The more I drink, the more they seem divine;
With joy elate my soul in love runs o'er,
And each fresh draught is sweeter than before.
Books bring me friends where'er on earth I be,—
Solace of solitude,—bonds of society!

I love my books! They are companions dear,
Sterling in worth, in friendship most sincere;
Here talk I with the wise in ages gone,
And with the nobly gifted of our own.
If love, joy, laughter, sorrow please my mind,
Love, joy, grief, laughter in my books I find.

## THE ART OF BOOK-KEEPING.

Laman Blanchard. *From his 'Poetical Works.' 1876.*

How hard, when those who do not wish
To lend, that's lose, their books,
Are snared by anglers—folks that fish
With literary hooks;

Who call and take some favorite tome,
But never read it through,—
They thus complete their set at home,
By making one at you.

Behold the bookshelf of a dunce
Who borrows—never lends:
Yon work, in twenty volumes, once
Belonged to twenty friends.

New tales and novels you may shut
From view—'tis all in vain;

They're gone—and though the leaves are "cut"
They never "come again."

For pamphlets lent I look around,
For tracts my tears are spilt;
But when they take a book that's bound,
'Tis surely extra-gilt.

A circulating library
Is mine—my birds are flown;
There's one odd volume left to be
Like all the rest, a-lone.

I, of my Spenser quite bereft,
Last winter sore was shaken;
Of Lamb I've but a quarter left,
Nor could I save my Bacon.

My Hall and Hill were levelled flat,
But Moore was still the cry;
And then, although I threw them Sprat,
They swallowed up my Pye.

O'er everything, however slight,
They seized some airy trammel;
They snatched my Hogg and Fox one night,
And pocketed my Campbell.

And then I saw my Crabbe at last,
Like Hamlet's, backward go;
And, as my tide was ebbing fast,
Of course I lost my Rowe.

I wondered into what balloon
My books their course had bent;
And yet, with all my marvelling, soon
I found my Marvell went.

My Mallet served to knock me down,
Which makes me thus a talker;
And once, while I was out of town,
My Johnson proved a Walker.

While studying o'er the fire one day
My Hobbes amidst the smoke,
They bore my Colman clean away,
And carried off my Coke.

They picked my Locke, to me far more
Than Bramah's patent's worth;
And now my losses I deplore
Without a Home on earth.

If once a book you let them lift,
Another they conceal;
For though I caught them stealing Swift,
As swiftly went my Steele.

Hope is not now upon my shelf,
Where late he stood elated;
But, what is strange, my Pope himself
Is excommunicated.

My little Suckling in the grave
Is sunk to swell the ravage;
And what 'twas Crusoe's fate to save
'Twas mine to lose—a Savage.

Even Glover's works I cannot put
My frozen hands upon;
Though ever since I lost my Foote
My Bunyan has been gone.

My Hoyle with Cotton went; oppressed,
My Taylor too must sail;
To save my Goldsmith from arrest,
In vain I offered Bayle.

I Prior sought, but could not see
The Hood so late in front;
And when I turned to hunt for Lee,
Oh! Where was my Leigh Hunt.

I tried to laugh, old Care to tickle,
Yet could not Tickell touch;
And then, alas! I missed my Mickle,
And surely mickle's much.

'Tis quite enough my griefs to feed,
My sorrows to excuse,
To think I cannot read my Reid,
Nor even use my Hughes.

To West, to South, I turn my head,
Exposed alike to odd jeers;
For since my Roger Ascham's fled,
I ask 'em for my Rogers.

They took my Horne—and Horne Tooke, too,
And thus my treasures flit;
I feel, when I would Hazlitt view,
The flames that it has lit.

My word's worth little, Wordsworth gone,
If I survive its doom;
How many a bard I doated on

Was swept off—with my Broome.

My classics would not quiet lie,
A thing so fondly hoped;
Like Dr. Primrose, I may cry,
"My Livy has eloped!"

My life is wasting fast away—
I suffer from these shocks;
And though I've fixed a lock on Gray,
There's gray upon my locks.

I'm far from young—am growing pale—
I see my Butter fly;
And when they ask about my *ail*,
'Tis Burton! I reply.

They still have made me slight returns,
And thus my griefs divide;
For oh! They've cured me of my Burns,
And eased my Akenside.

But all I think I shall not say,
Nor let my anger burn;
For as they never found me Gay,
They have not left me Sterne.

## IN THE LIBRARY.

ANNE C. L. BOTTA. *From her collected 'Poems.' 1882.*

Speak low—tread softly through these halls;
Here genius lives enshrined,—
Here reign, in silent majesty,
The monarchs of the mind.

A mighty spirit-host, they come
From every age and clime;
Above the buried wrecks of years
They breast the tide of time.

And in their presence-chamber here
They hold their regal state,
And round them throng a noble train,
The gifted and the great.

O child of earth, when round thy path
The storms of life arise,
And when thy brothers pass thee by
With stern, unloving eyes,—

Here shall the Poets chant for thee

Their sweetest, loftiest lays;
And Prophets wait to guide thy steps
In wisdom's pleasant ways.

Come, with these God-anointed kings
Be thou companion here,
And in the mighty realm of mind
Thou shalt go forth a peer.

## MY SHAKSPERE[2].

H. C. BUNNER.  *Written expressly for this collection.*

With bevelled binding, with uncut edge,
With broad white margin and gilded top,
Fit for my library's choicest ledge,
Fresh from the bindery, smelling of shop,
In tinted cloth, with a strange design—
Buskin and scroll-work and mask and crown,
And an arabesque legend tumbling down—
"The Works of Shakspere" were never so fine.
Fresh from the shop! I turn the page—
Its "ample margin" is wide and fair—
Its type is chosen with daintiest care;
There's a "New French Elzevir" strutting there
That would shame its prototypic age.
Fresh from the shop! O Shakspere mine,
I've half a notion you're much too fine!

There's an ancient volume that I recall,
In foxy leather much chafed and worn;
Its back is broken by many a fall,
The stitches are loose and the leaves are torn;
And gone is the bastard-title, next
To the title-page scribbled with owners' names,
That in straggling old-style type proclaims
That the work is from the corrected text
Left by the late Geo. Steevens, Esquire.

The broad sky burns like a great blue fire,
And the Lake shines blue as shimmering steel,
And it cuts the horizon like a blade—
But behind the poplar's a strip of shade—
The great tall Lombardy on the lawn.
And lying there in the grass, I feel
The wind that blows from the Canada shore,
And in cool, sweet puffs comes stealing o'er,
Fresh as any October dawn.

---
[2] The poems thus marked were written or translated for the present collection.

I lie on my breast in the grass, my feet
Lifted boy-fashion, and swinging free,
The old brown Shakspere in front of me.
And big are my eyes, and my heart's a-beat;
And my whole soul's lost—in what?—who knows?
Perdita's charms or Perdita's woes—
Perdita fairy-like, fair and sweet.
Is any one jealous, I wonder, now,
Of my love for Perdita? For I vow
I loved her well. And who can say
That life would be quite the same life to-day—
That Love would mean so much, if she
Had not taught me its A B C?

The Grandmother, thin and bent and old,
But her hair still dark and her eyes still bright,
Totters around among her flowers—
Old-fashioned flowers of pink and white;
And turns with a trowel the dark rich mould
That feeds the blooms of her heart's delight.
Ah me! for her and for me the hours
Go by, and for her the smell of earth—
And for me the breeze and a far love's birth,
And the sun and the sky and all the things
That a boy's heart hopes and a poet sings.

Fresh from the shop! O Shakspere mine,
It wasn't the binding made you divine!
I knew you first in a foxy brown,
In the old, old home, where I laid me down,
In the idle summer afternoons,
With you alone in the odorous grass,
And set your thoughts to the wind's low tunes,
And saw your children rise up and pass—
And dreamed and dreamed of the things to be,
Known only, I think, to you and me.

I've hardly a heart for you dressed so fine—
Fresh from the shop, O Shakspere mine!

## THE BOOKWORMS.

Robert Burns.

*Burns saw a splendidly bound but sadly neglected copy of Shakspere in the library of a nobleman in Edinburgh, and he wrote these lines on the ample margin of one of its pages, where they were found long after the poet's death.*

Through and through the inspired leaves,
Ye maggots, make your windings;
But oh, respect his lordship's taste,
And spare the golden bindings.

## CATULLUS TO HIS BOOK.[3]
### QVOI DONO LEPIDVM NOVVM LIBELLVM.

Caius Valerius Catullus. *Translated by A. Lang expressly for this collection.*

My little book, that's neat and new,
Fresh polished with dry pumice stone,
To whom, Cornelius, but to you,
Shall *this* be sent, for you alone—
(Who used to praise my lines, my own)—
Have dared, in weighty volumes three,
(What labors, Jove, what learning thine!)
To tell the Tale of Italy,
And all the legend of our line.

So take, whate'er its worth may be,
My Book,—but Lady and Queen of Song,
This one kind gift I crave of thee,
That it may live for ages long!

## OLD BOOKS ARE BEST.
### TO
### J. H. P.

Beverly Chew. *From the 'Critic' of March 13, 1886.*

Old Books are best! With what delight
Does "Faithorne fecit" greet our sight
On frontispiece or title-page
Of that old time, when on the stage
"Sweet Nell" set "Rowley's" heart alight!

And you, O Friend, to whom I write,
Must not deny, e'en though you might,
Through fear of modern pirate's rage,
Old Books are best.

What though the prints be not so bright,
The paper dark, the binding slight?
Our author, be he dull or sage,
Returning from that distant age

---

[3] The poems thus marked were written or translated for the present collection.

So lives again, we say of right:
Old Books are best.

## THE FORGOTTEN BOOKS.[4]

THOMAS S. COLLIER. *Written expressly for this collection.*

Hid by the garret's dust, and lost
Amid the cobwebs wreathed above,
They lie, these volumes that have cost
Such weeks of hope and waste of love.

The Theologian's garnered lore
Of Scripture text, and words divine;
And verse, that to some fair one bore
Thoughts that like fadeless stars would shine;

The grand wrought epics, that were born
From mighty throes of heart and brain,—
Here rest, their covers all unworn,
And all their pages free from stain.

Here lie the chronicles that told
Of man, and his heroic deeds—
Alas! the words once "writ in gold"
Are tarnished so that no one reads.

And tracts that smote each other hard,
While loud the friendly plaudits rang,
All animosities discard,
Where old, moth-eaten garments hang.

The heroes that were made to strut
In tinsel on "life's mimic stage"
Found, all too soon, the deepening rut
Which kept them silent in the page;

And heroines, whose loveless plight
Should wake the sympathetic tear,
In volumes sombre as the night
Sleep on through each succeeding year.

Here Phyllis languishes forlorn,
And Strephon waits beside his flocks,
And early huntsmen wind the horn,
Within the boundaries of a box.

Here, by the irony of fate,
Beside the "peasant's humble board,"
The monarch "flaunts his robes of state,"
And spendthrifts find the miser's hoard.

---

[4] The poems thus marked were written or translated for the present collection.

Days come and go, and still we write,
And hope for some far happier lot
Than that our work should meet this blight—
And yet—some books must be forgot.

## AN INVOCATION IN A LIBRARY.

Helen Gray Cone. *From 'Oberon and Puck.' 1885.*

O brotherhood, with bay-crowned brows undaunted,
Who passed serene along our crowded ways,
Speak with us still! For we, like Saul, are haunted:
Harp sullen spirits from these later days!

Whate'er high hope ye had for man your brother,
Breathe it, nor leave him, like a prisoned slave,
To stare through bars upon a sight no other
Than clouded skies that lighten on a grave.

In these still alcoves give us gentle meeting,
From dusky shelves kind arms about us fold,
Till the New Age shall feel her cold heart beating
Restfully on the warm heart of the Old:

Till we shall hear your voices, mild and winning
Steal through our doubt and discord, as outswells
At fiercest noon, above a city's dinning,
The chiming music of cathedral bells:

Music that lifts the thought from trodden places,
And coarse confusions that around us lie,
Up to the calm of high, cloud-silvered spaces,
Where the tall spire points through the soundless sky.

## CONCERNING THE HONOR OF BOOKS.

Samuel Daniel. *This sonnet, prefixed to the second edition of Florio's Montaigne, 1613, is generally attributed to the translator, but the best critics now incline to the belief that it is by his friend, Daniel.*

Since honor from the honorer proceeds,
How well do they deserve, that memorize
And leave in books for all posterity
The names of worthies and their virtuous deeds;
When all their glory else, like water-weeds
Without their element, presently dies,
And all their greatness quite forgotten lies,

And when and how they flourished no man heeds;
How poor remembrances are statues, tombs,
And other monuments that men erect
To princes, which remain in closèd rooms,
Where but a few behold them, in respect
Of books, that to the universal eye
Show how they lived; the other where they lie!

## LINES.

Isaac D'Israeli. *Imitated from Rantzau, the founder of the library at Copenhagen.*

Golden volumes! richest treasures!
Objects of delicious pleasures!
You my eyes rejoicing please,
You my hands in rapture seize!
Brilliant wits, and musing sages,
Lights who beamed through many ages,
Left to your conscious leaves their story,
And dared to trust you with their glory;
And now their hope of fame achieved!
Dear volumes! you have not deceived!

## MY BOOKS.

Austin Dobson. *From 'At the Sign of the Lyre.' 1885.*

They dwell in the odor of camphor,
They stand in a Sheraton shrine,
They are "warranted early editions,"
These worshipful tomes of mine;—

In their creamy "Oxford vellum,"
In their redolent "crushed Levant,"
With their delicate watered linings,
They are jewels of price, I grant;—

Blind-tooled and morocco-jointed,
They have Bedford's daintiest dress,
They are graceful, attenuate, polished,
But they gather the dust, no less;—

For the row that I prize is yonder,
Away on the unglazed shelves,
The bulged and the bruised *octavos*,
The dear and the dumpy twelves,—

Montaigne with his sheepskin blistered,
And Howell the worse for wear,

And the worm-drilled Jesuits' Horace,
And the little old cropped Molière,—

And the Burton I bought for a florin,
And the Rabelais foxed and flea'd,—
For the others I never have opened,
But those are the ones I read.

## TO A MISSAL OF THE THIRTEENTH CENTURY.

AUSTIN DOBSON. *From 'At the Sign of the Lyre.' 1885.*

Missal of the Gothic age,
Missal with the blazoned page,
Whence, O Missal, hither come,
From what dim scriptorium?

Whose the name that wrought thee thus,
Ambrose or Theophilus,
Bending, through the waning light,
O'er thy vellum scraped and white;

Weaving 'twixt thy rubric lines
Sprays and leaves and quaint designs:
Setting round thy border scrolled
Buds of purple and of gold?

Ah!—a wondering brotherhood,
Doubtless, round that artist stood,
Strewing o'er his careful ways
Little choruses of praise;

Glad when his deft hand would paint
Strife of Sathanas and Saint,
Or in secret coign entwist
Jest of cloister humorist.

Well the worker earned his wage,
Bending o'er the blazoned page!
Tired the hand and tired the wit
Ere the final *Explicit*!

Not as ours the books of old—
Things that steam can stamp and fold;
Not as ours the books of yore—
Rows of type, and nothing more.

Then a book was still a Book,
Where a wistful man might look,
Finding something through the whole,
Beating—like a human soul.

In that growth of day by day,
When to labor was to pray,
Surely something vital passed
To the patient page at last;

Something that one still perceives
Vaguely present in the leaves;
Something from the worker lent;
Something mute—but eloquent!

## THE BOOK-PLATE'S PETITION.
### BY A GENTLEMAN OF THE TEMPLE.

AUSTIN DOBSON. *Published originally in 'Notes and Queries,' January 8, 1881.*

While cynic CHARLES still trimm'd the vane
'Twixt *Querouaille* and *Castlemaine*,
In days that shocked JOHN EVELYN,
My First Possessor fix'd me in.
In days of *Dutchmen* and of frost,
The narrow sea with JAMES I crossed;
Returning when once more began
The Age of *Saturn* and of ANNE.
I am a part of all the past;
I knew the GEORGES, first and last;
I have been oft where else was none
Save the great wig of ADDISON;
And seen on shelves beneath me grope
The little eager form of POPE.
I lost the Third that own'd me when
French NOAILLES fled at Dettingen;
The year JAMES WOLFE surpris'd Quebec,
The Fourth in hunting broke his neck;
The day that WILLIAM HOGARTH dy'd,
The Fifth one found me in Cheapside.

This was a *Scholar*, one of those
Whose *Greek* is sounder than their *hose*;
He lov'd old books, and nappy ale,
So liv'd at Streatham, next to THRALE.
'Twas there this stain of grease I boast
Was made by DR. JOHNSON's toast.
(He did it, as I think, for spite;
My Master called him *Jacobite*!)
And now that I so long to-day
Have rested *post discrimina*,

Safe in the brass-wir'd book-case where
I watched the Vicar's whit'ning hair
Must I these travell'd bones inter
In some *Collector's* sepulchre!
Must I be torn from hence and thrown
With *frontispiece* and *colophon*!
With vagrant *E*'s, and *I*'s and *O*'s,
The spoil of plunder'd *Folios*!
With scraps and snippets that to Me
Are naught but *kitchen company*!
Nay, rather, Friend, this favor grant me;
Tear me at once; *but don't transplant me.*

CHELTENHAM,
*Sept. 31, 1792.*

## OVER THE THRESHOLD OF MY LIBRARY.

HENRY DRURY.

*Quoted from the supplement of Dibdin's 'Bibliomania,' where the original Latin lines may be found.*

From mouldering Abbey's dark Scriptorium brought,
See vellum tomes by Monkish labor wrought;
Nor yet the comma born, Papyri see,
And uncial letters' wizard grammary:
View my *fifteeners* in their ragged line;
What ink! What linen! Only known long syne—
Entering where Aldus might have fixed his throne,
Or Harry Stephens coveted his own.

## THE CHRYSALIS OF A BOOKWORM.

MAURICE F. EGAN.　　　　　　　　　　*From 'Songs and Sonnets.' 1885.*

I read, O friend, no pages of old lore,
Which I loved well, and yet the flying days,
That softly passed as wind through green spring ways
And left a perfume, swift fly as of yore,
Though in clear Plato's stream I look no more,
Neither with Moschus sing Sicilian lays,
Nor with bold Dante wander in amaze,
Nor see our Will the Golden Age restore.
I read a book to which old books are new,
And new books old. A living book is mine—
In age, three years: in it I read no lies—
In it to myriad truths I find the clew—
A tender, little child: but I divine

Thoughts high as Dante's in its clear blue eyes.

## EPIGRAM.

Evenus (the grammarian). *Rendered into English by A. Lang in the 'Library.' 1881.*

Pest of the Muses, devourer of pages, in crannies hat lurkest,
Fruits of the Muses to taint, labor of learning to spoil;
Wherefore, O black-fleshed worm! wert thou born for the evil thou workest?
Wherefore thine own foul form shap'st thou with envious toil?

## THE BIBLIOMANIA.

Hic, inquis, veto quisquam fuit oletum.
Pinge duos angues.
Pers. *Sat.* i. l. 108.

John Ferriar. *"An Epistle to Richard Heber, Esq." Manchester, April, 1809.*

What wild desires, what restless torments seize
The hapless man, who feels the book-disease,
If niggard Fortune cramp his gen'rous mind
And Prudence quench the Spark by heaven assign'd!
With wistful glance his aching eyes behold
The Princeps-copy, clad in blue and gold,
Where the tall Book-case, with partition thin,
Displays, yet guards the tempting charms within:
So great Facardin view'd, as sages[5] tell,
Fair Crystalline immur'd in lucid cell.

Not thus the few, by happier fortune grac'd,
And blest, like you, with talents, wealth, and taste,
Who gather nobly, with judicious hand,
The Muse's treasures from each letter'd strand.
For you the Monk illum'd his pictur'd page,
For you the press defies the Spoils of age;
Faustus for you infernal tortures bore,

For you Erasmus[6] starv'd on Adria's shore.
The Folio-Aldus loads your happy Shelves,
And dapper Elzevirs, like fairy elves,
Shew their light forms amidst the well-gilt Twelves:

---

[5] *Sages*, Count Hamilton, in the 'Quatre Facardins,' and Mr. M. Lewis, in his 'Tales of Romance.'

[6] See the 'Opulentia Sordida,' in his 'Colloquies,' where he complains feelingly of the spare Venetian diet.

In slender type the Giolitos shine,
And bold Bodoni stamps his Roman line.
For you the Louvre opes its regal doors,
And either Didot lends his brilliant stores:
With faultless types, and costly sculptures bright,
Ibarra's Quixote charms your ravish'd sight:
Laborde in splendid tablets shall explain
Thy beauties, glorious, tho' unhappy Spain!
O, hallowed name, the theme of future years,
Embalm'd in Patriot-blood, and England's tears,
Be thine fresh honors from the tuneful tongue,
By Isis' stream which mourning Zion sung!

But devious oft' from ev'ry classic Muse,
The keen Collector meaner paths will choose:
And first the Margin's breadth his soul employs,
Pure, snowy, broad, the type of nobler joys.
In vain might Homer roll the tide of song,
Or Horace smile, or Tully charm the throng;
If crost by Pallas' ire, the trenchant blade
Or too oblique, or near, the edge invade,
The Bibliomane exclaims, with haggard eye,
"No Margin!" turns in haste, and scorns to buy.
He turns where Pybus rears his Atlas-head,
Or Madoc's mass conceals its veins of lead.
The glossy lines in polish'd order stand,
While the vast margin spreads on either hand,
Like Russian wastes, that edge the frozen deep, Chill with pale
glare, and lull to mortal sleep.[7]

Or English books, neglected and forgot,
Excite his wish in many a dusty lot:
Whatever trash *Midwinter* gave to day,
Or *Harper's* rhiming sons, in paper gray,
At ev'ry auction, bent on fresh supplies,
He cons his Catalogue with anxious eyes:
Where'er the slim Italics mark the page,
*Curious and rare* his ardent mind engage.
Unlike the Swans, in Tuscan Song display'd,
He hovers eager o'er Oblivion's Shade,
To snatch obscurest names from endless night,

---

[7] It may be said that Quintilian recommends margins; but it is with a view to their being occasionally occupied: Debet vacare etiam locus, in quo notentur quæ scribentibus solent extra ordinem, id est ex aliis quam qui sunt in manibus loci, occurrere. Irrumpunt enim optimi nonnunquam Sensus, quos neque inserere oportet, neque differre tutum est. 'Instit.' lib. x. c. 3.

He was therefore no *Margin-man*, in the modern sense.

And give Cokain or Fletcher[8] back to light.
In red morocco drest he loves to boast
The bloody murder, or the yelling ghost;
Or dismal ballads, sung to crouds of old,
Now cheaply bought for thrice their weight in gold.
Yet to th' unhonor'd dead be Satire just;
Some flow'rs[9] "smell sweet and blossom in their dust."
'Tis thus ev'n Shirley boasts a golden line,
And Lovelace strikes, by fits, a note divine.
Th' unequal gleams like midnight-lightnings play,
And deepen'd gloom succeeds, in place of day.

But human bliss still meets some envious storm;
He droops to view his Paynters' mangled form:
Presumptuous grief, while pensive Taste repines
O'er the frail relics of her Attic Shrines!
O for that power, for which Magicians vye.
To look through earth, and secret hoards descry!
I'd spurn such gems as Marinel[10] beheld,
And all the wealth Aladdin's cavern held,
Might I divine in what mysterious gloom
The rolls of sacred bards have found their tomb:
Beneath what mould'ring tower, or waste champain,
Is hid Menander, sweetest of the train:
Where rests Antimachus' forgotten lyre,
Where gentle Sappho's still seductive fire;
Or he,[11] whom chief the laughing Muses own,
Yet skill'd with softest accents to bemoan
Sweet Philomel[12] in strains so like her own.

The menial train has prov'd the Scourge of wit,
Ev'n Omar burnt less Science than the spit.
Earthquakes and wars remit their deadly rage,
But ev'ry feast demands some fated page.

---

[8] *Fletcher.* A translator of Martial. A very bad Poet, but *exceedingly scarce*.
[9] Only the actions of the just
    Smell sweet, and blossom in the dust.

Shirley.

Perhaps Shirley had in view this passage of Persius,—
    Nunc non é tumulo, fortunataque favilla
    Nascentur Violæ?

'Sat.' i. l. 37.

[10] 'Faërie Queene.'
[11] Aristophanes.
[12] See his exquisite hymn to the Nightingale in his **Ornithes**.

Ye Towers of Julius,[13] ye alone remain
Of all the piles that saw our nation's stain,
When HARRY's sway opprest the groaning realm,
And Lust and Rapine seiz'd the wav'ring helm.
Then ruffian-hands defaced the sacred fanes,
Their saintly statues and their storied panes;
Then from the chest, with ancient art embost,
The Penman's pious scrolls were rudely tost;
Then richest manuscripts, profusely spread,
The brawny Churls' devouring Oven fed:
And thence Collectors date the heav'nly ire
That wrapt Augusta's domes in sheets of fire.[14]

Taste, tho' misled, may yet some purpose gain,
But Fashion guides a book-compelling train.[15]
Once, far apart from Learning's moping crew,
The travell'd beau display'd his red-heel'd shoe,
Till ORFORD rose, and told of rhiming Peers,
Repeating *noble* words to polish'd ears;[16]
Taught the gay croud to prize a fluttering name,
In trifling toil'd, nor "blush'd to find it fame."
The letter'd fop, now takes a larger scope,
With classic furniture, design'd by HOPE,
(HOPE whom Upholst'rers eye with mute despair,
The doughty pedant of an elbow-chair;)
Now warm'd by ORFORD, and by GRANGER school'd,
In Paper-books, superbly gilt and tool'd,
He pastes, from injur'd volumes snipt away,
His *English Heads*, in chronicled array.
Torn from their destin'd page (unworthy meed
Of knightly counsel, and heroic deed)
Not FAITHORNE's stroke, nor FIELD's own types can save[17] The
gallant Veres, and one-eyed OGLE brave.
Indignant readers seek the image fled,
And curse the busy fool, who *wants a head*.

Proudly he shews, with many a smile elate,
The scrambling subjects of the *private plate*;

---

[13] Gray.
[14] The fire of London.
[15] Cloud-compelling Jove.—Pope's 'Iliad.'
[16] ... gaudent prænomine molles
 Auriculæ.

JUVENAL.

[17] *The gallant Veres and one-eyed Ogle.* Three fine heads, for the sake of which, the beautiful and interesting 'Commentaries' of Sir Francis Veres have been mutilated by the Collectors of English portraits.

While Time their actions and their names bereaves,
They grin for ever in the guarded leaves.

Like Poets, born, in vain Collectors strive
To cross their Fate, and learn the art to thrive.
Like Cacus, bent to tame their struggling will,
The Tyrant-passion drags them backward still:
Ev'n I, debarr'd of ease, and studious hours,
Confess, mid' anxious toil, its lurking pow'rs.
How pure the joy, when first my hands unfold
The small, rare volume, black with tarnish'd gold!
The Eye skims restless, like the roving bee,
O'er flowers of wit, or song, or repartee,
While sweet as Springs, new-bubbling from the stone,
Glides through the breast some pleasing theme unknown.

Now dipt in ROSSI's[18] terse and classic style,
His harmless tales awake a transient smile.
Now BOUCHET's motley stores my thoughts arrest,
With wond'rous reading, and with learned jest.
Bouchet[19] whose tomes a grateful line demand,
The valued gift of STANLEY's lib'ral hand.
Now sadly pleased, through faded Rome I stray,
And mix regrets with gentle DU BELLAY;[20]
Or turn, with keen delight, the curious page,
Where hardy Pasquin[21] braves the Pontiff's rage.

But D——n's strains should tell the sad reverse,
When Business calls, invet'rate foe to verse!
Tell how "the Demon claps his iron hands,"
"Waves his lank locks, and scours along the lands."
Through wintry blasts, or summer's fire I go,
To scenes of danger, and to sights of woe.
Ev'n when to Margate ev'ry Cockney roves,
And brainsick-poets long for shelt'ring groves,
Whose lofty shades exclude the noontide glow,
While Zephyrs breathe, and waters trill below,[22]
Me rigid Fate averts, by tasks like these,

---

[18] Generally known by the name of James Nicius Erythræus. The allusion is to his 'Pinacotheca.'

[19] 'Les Serées de Gillaume Bouchet,' a book of uncommon rarity. I possess a handsome copy by the kindness of Colonel Stanley.

[20] 'Les Regrets,' by Joachim du Bellay, contain a most amusing and instructive account of Rome in the sixteenth century.

[21] 'Pasquillorum Tomi duo.'

[22] Errare per lucos, æmænæ,
    Quos et aquæ subeunt et auræ.

HORAT.

From heav'nly musings, and from letter'd ease.

Such wholesome checks the better Genius sends,
From dire rehearsals to protect our friends:
Else when the social rites our joys renew,
The stuff'd Portfolio would alarm your view,
Whence volleying rhimes your patience would o'er-come,
And, spite of kindness, drive you early home.
So when the traveller's hasty footsteps glide
Near smoking lava on Vesuvio's side,
Hoarse-mutt'ring thunders from the depths proceed,
And spouting fires incite his eager speed.
Appall'd he flies, while rattling show'rs invade,
Invoking ev'ry Saint for instant aid:
Breathless, amaz'd, he seeks the distant shore,
And vows to tempt the dang'rous gulph no more.

### TRIOLET TO HER HUSBAND.

F. FERTIAULT. *Rendered into English by A. Lang in the 'Library.' 1881.*

Books rule thy mind, so let it be!
Thy heart is mine, and mine alone.
What more can I require of thee?
Books rule thy mind, so let it be!
Contented when thy bliss I see,
I wish a world of books thine own.
Books rule thy mind, so let it be!
Thy heart is mine, and mine alone.

### A NOOK AND A BOOK.

WILLIAM FREELAND. *From 'A Birth Song and other Poems.' 1882.*

Give me a nook and a book,
And let the proud world spin round;
Let it scramble by hook or by crook
For wealth or a name with a sound.
You are welcome to amble your ways,
Aspirers to place or to glory;
May big bells jangle your praise,
And golden pens blazon your story!
For me, let me dwell in my nook,
Here by the curve of this brook,
That croons to the tune of my book,
Whose melody wafts me forever

On the waves of an unseen river.

Give me a book and a nook
Far away from the glitter and strife;
Give me a staff and a crook,
The calm and the sweetness of life;
Let me pause—let me brood as I list,
On the marvels of heaven's own spinning—
Sunlight and moonlight and mist,
Glorious without slaying or sinning.
Vain world, let me reign in my nook,
King of this kingdom, my book,
A region by fashion forsook;
Pass on, ye lean gamblers for glory,
Nor mar the sweet tune of my story!

## THE SULTAN OF MY BOOKS.[23]

*There is many a true word spoken in doggerel.— Czech Folk-Song.*

Edmund Gosse. *Written for the present collection.*

Come hither, my Wither,
My Suckling, my Dryden!
My Hudibras, hither!
My Heinsius from Leyden!
Dear Play-books in quarto,
Fat tomes in brown leather,
Stray never too far to
Come back here together!

Books writ on occult and
Heretical letters,
I, I am the Sultan
Of you and your betters.
I need you all round me;
When wits have grown muddy,
My best hours have found me
With you in my study.

I've varied departments
To give my books shelter;
Shelves, open apartments
For tomes helter-skelter;
There are artisans' flats, fit
For common editions,—
I find them, as that's fit,
Good wholesome positions.

---

[23] The poems thus marked were written or translated for the present collection.

But books that I cherish
Live under glass cases;
In the waste lest they perish
I build them oases;
Where gas cannot find them,
Where worms cannot grapple,
Those panes hold behind them,
My eye and its apple.

And here you see flirting
Fine folks of distinction:
Unique books just skirting
The verge of extinction;
Old texts with one error
And long notes upon it;
The 'Magistrates' Mirror'
(With Nottingham's sonnet);

Tooled Russias to gaze on,
Moroccos to fondle,
My Denham, in blazon,
My vellum-backed Vondel,
My Marvell,—a copy
Was never seen taller,—
My Jones's 'Love's Poppy,'
My dear little Waller;

My Sandys, a real jewel!
My exquisite, 'Adamo!'
My Dean Donne's 'Death's Duel!'
My Behn (naughty madam O!);
Ephelia's! Orinda's!
Ma'am Pix and Ma'am Barker!—
The rhymsters you find, as
The morals grow darker!

I never upbraid these
Old periwigged sinners,
Their songs and light ladies,
Their dances and dinners;
My book-shelf's a haven
From storms puritanic,—
We sure may be gay when
Of death we've no panic!

My parlor is little,
And poor are its treasures;
All pleasures are brittle,
And so are my pleasures;

But though I shall never
Be Beckford or Locker,
While Fate does not sever
The door from the knocker,

No book shall tap vainly
At latch or at lattice
(If costumed urbanely,
And worth our care, that is):
My poets from slumber
Shall rise in morocco,
To shield the new comer
From storm or sirocco.

—————————

I might prate thus for pages,
The theme is so pleasant;
But the gloom of the ages
Lies on me at present;
All business and fear to
The cold world I banish.
Hush! like the Ameer, to
My harem I vanish!

## OUR BOOK-SHELVES.

THOMAS GORDON HAKE. *From the 'State' of April 17, 1886.*

What solace would those books afford,
In gold and vellum cover,
Could men but say them word for word
Who never turn them over!

Books that must know themselves by heart
As by endowment vital,
Could they their truths to us impart
Not stopping with the title!

Line after line their wisdom flows,
Page after page repeating;
Yet never on our ears bestows
A single sound of greeting.

As thus they lie upon the shelves,
Such wisdom in their pages,
Do they rehearse it to themselves,
Or rest like silent sages?

One book we know such fun invokes,
As well were worth the telling:

Must it not chuckle o'er the jokes
That it is ever spelling?

And for the Holy Bible there,
It greets us with mild teaching;
Though no one its contents may hear,
Does it not go on preaching?

## TO HIS BOOK.

ROBERT HERRICK. *Prefixed to 'Hesperides.' 1648.*

While thou didst keep thy candor undefiled,
Dearly I loved thee, as my first-born child;
But when I sent thee wantonly to roam
From house to house, and never stay at home;
I brake my bonds of love, and bade thee go,
Regardless whether well thou sped'st or no,
On with thy fortunes then, whate'er they be;
If good I'll smile, if bad I'll sigh for thee.

## TO HIS BOOK.

ROBERT HERRICK.

Make haste away, and let one be
A friendly patron unto thee;
Lest, rapt from hence, I see thee lie
Torn for the use of pastery;
Or see thy injured leaves serve well
To make loose gowns for mackerel;
Or see the grocers, in a trice,
Make hoods of thee to serve out spice.

## TO HIS BOOKS.[24]

Q. HORATIUS FLACCUS. *Imitated by Austin Dobson from the 'Epistles,' i. 20, for the present collection.*

For mart and street you seem to pine
With restless glances, Book of mine!
Still craving on some stall to stand,
Fresh pumiced from the binder's hand.
You chafe at locks, and burn to quit
Your modest haunt and audience fit,
For hearers less discriminate.

---

[24] The poems thus marked were written or translated for the present collection.

I reared you up for no such fate.
Still, if you *must* be published, go;
But mind, you can't come back, you know!

"What have I done?"—I hear you cry,
And writhe beneath some critic's eye;
'What did I want?'—when, scarce polite,
They do but yawn, and roll you tight.
And yet, methinks, if I may guess
(Putting aside your heartlessness
In leaving me, and this your home),
You should find favor, too, at Rome.
That is, they'll like you while you're young.
When you are old, you'll pass among
The Great Unwashed,—then thumbed and sped,
Be fretted of slow moths, unread,
Or to Ilerda you'll be sent,
Or Utica, for banishment!
And I, whose counsel you disdain,
At that your lot shall laugh amain,
Wryly, as he who, like a fool,
Pushed o'er the cliff his restive mule.
Stay, there is worse behind. In age
They e'en may take your babbling page
In some remotest "slum" to teach
Mere boys the rudiments of speech!
But go. When on warm days you see
A chance of listeners, speak of me.
Tell them I soared from low estate,
A freedman's son, to higher fate
(That is, make up to me in worth
What you must take in point of birth);
Then tell them that I won renown
In peace and war, and pleased the Town;
Paint me as early gray, and one
Little of stature, fond of sun,
Quick-tempered, too,—but nothing more.
Add (if they ask) I'm forty-four,
Or was, the year that over us
Both Lollius ruled and Lepidus.

## SONNET.

Leigh Hunt.

*Found by Mr. Alexander Ireland in the London 'Examiner' of December 24, 1815, and not anywhere included in the poet's collected works.*

Were I to name, out of the times gone by,
The poets dearest to me, I should say,
Pulci for spirits, and a fine, free way;
Chaucer for manners, and close, silent eye;
Milton for classic taste, and harp strung high;
Spenser for luxury, and sweet, sylvan play;
Horace for chatting with, from day to day;
Shakspere for all, but most society.

But which take with me, could I take but one?
Shakspere, as long as I was unoppressed
With the world's weight, making sad thoughts intenser;
But did I wish, out of the common sun,
To lay a wounded heart in leafy rest,
And dream of things far off and healing,—Spenser.

## MY BOOKS.

WILLIS FLETCHER JOHNSON. *From the Boston 'Transcript.'*

On my study shelves they stand,
Well known all to eye and hand,
Bound in gorgeous cloth of gold,
In morocco rich and old.
Some in paper, plain and cheap,
Some in muslin, calf, and sheep;
Volumes great and volumes small,
Ranged along my study wall;
But their contents are past finding
By their size or by their binding.

There is one with gold agleam,
Like the Sangreal in a dream,
Back and boards in every part
Triumph of the binder's art;
Costing more, 'tis well believed,
Than the author e'er received.
But its contents? Idle tales,
Flappings of a shallop's sails!
In the treasury of learning
Scarcely worth a penny's turning.

Here's a tome in paper plain,
Soiled and torn and marred with stain,
Cowering from each statelier book
In the darkest, dustiest nook.
Take it down, and lo! each page
Breathes the wisdom of a sage:
Weighed a thousand times in gold,

Half its worth would not be told,
For all truth of ancient story
Crowns each line with deathless glory.

On my study shelves they stand;
But my study walls expand,
As thought's pinions are unfurled,
Till they compass all the world.
Endless files go marching by,
Men of lowly rank and high,
Some in broadcloth, gem-adorned,
Some in homespun, fortune-scorned;
But God's scales that all are weighed in
Heed not what each man's arrayed in!

## TO MY BOOKSELLER.

BEN JONSON.

*This is from the third of the poet's books of epigrams. Bucklersbury was the street most affected by grocers and apothecaries.*

Thou that mak'st gain thy end, and wisely well,
Call'st a book good, or bad, as it doth sell,
Use mine so too; I give thee leave; but crave,
For the luck's sake, it thus much favor have,
To lie upon thy stall, till it be sought;
Not offered, as it made suit to be bought;
Nor have my title-leaf on posts or walls,
Or in cleft-sticks, advanced to make calls
For termers, or some clerk-like serving-man,
Who scarce can spell thy hard names; whose knight less can.
If without these vile arts it will not sell,
Send it to Bucklersbury, there 't will well.

## TO SIR HENRY GOODYERE.

BEN JONSON.

*This is the eighty-sixth of the poet's first book of epigrams, and, like its immediate predecessor, it was addressed to a gentleman bound in bonds of friendship to many of the men of genius of his time.*

When I would know thee, Goodyere, my thought looks
Upon thy well-made choice of friends and books;
Then do I love thee, and behold thy ends
In making thy friends books, and thy books friends:

Now must I give thy life and deed the voice
Attending such a study, such a choice;
Where, though 't be love that to thy praise doth move,
It was a knowledge that begat that love.

## IN THE ALBUM OF LUCY BARTON.

CHARLES LAMB. *Written in 1824 for the daughter of his friend Bernard Barton.*

Little Book, surnamed of *white*,
Clean as yet and fair to sight,
Keep thy attribution right.

Never disproportioned scrawl;
Ugly blot, that's worse than all;
On thy maiden clearness fall!

In each letter, here designed,
Let the reader emblemed find
Neatness of the owner's mind.

Gilded margins count a sin,
Let thy leaves attraction win
By the golden rules within;

Saying fetched from sages old;
Laws which Holy Writ unfold,
Worthy to be graved in gold:

Lighter fancies not excluding;
Blameless wit, with nothing rude in,
Sometimes mildly interluding,

Amid strains of graver measure:
Virtue's self hath oft her pleasure
In sweet Muses' groves of leisure.

Riddles dark, perplexing sense;
Darker meanings of offence;
What but *shades*—he banished hence.

Whitest thoughts in whitest dress,
Candid meanings, best express
Mind of quiet Quakeress.

## BALLADE OF THE BOOK-HUNTER.

A. LANG. *From 'Ballades in Blue China.' 1880.*

In torrid heats of late July,
In March, beneath the bitter *bise*,

He book-hunts while the loungers fly,—
He book-hunts, though December freeze;
In breeches baggy at the knees,
And heedless of the public jeers,
For these, for these, he hoards his fees,
Aldines, Bodonis, Elzevirs.

No dismal stall escapes his eye,
He turns o'er tomes of low degrees,
There soiled Romanticists may lie,
Or Restoration comedies;
Each tract that flutters in the breeze
For him is charged with hopes and fears,
In mouldy novels fancy sees
Aldines, Bodonis, Elzevirs!

With restless eyes that peer and spy,
Sad eyes that heed not skies nor trees,
In dismal nooks he loves to pry,
Whose motto evermore is *Spes*!
But ah! the fabled treasure flees;
Grown rarer with the fleeting years,
In rich men's shelves they take their ease,
Aldines, Bodonis, Elzevirs!

ENVOY.

Prince, all the things that tease and please,
Fame, love, wealth, kisses, cheers, and tears,
What are they but such toys as these—
Aldines, Bodonis, Elzevirs?

## BALLADE OF TRUE WISDOM.

A. LANG.  *From 'Ballades in Blue China.' 1880.*

While others are asking for beauty or fame,
Or praying to know that for which they should pray,
Or courting Queen Venus, that affable dame,
Or chasing the Muses the weary and gray,
The sage has found out a more excellent way,—
To Pan and to Pallas his incense he showers,
And his humble petition puts up day by day,
For a house full of books, and a garden of flowers.

Inventors may bow to the God that is lame,
And crave from the light of his stithy a ray;
Philosophers kneel to the God without name,
Like the people of Athens, agnostics are they;
The hunter a fawn to Diana will slay,

The maiden wild roses will wreathe for the Hours,—
But the wise man will ask, ere libation he pay,
For a house full of books, and a garden of flowers.

Oh grant me a life without pleasure or blame
(As mortals count pleasure who rush through their day
With a speed to which that of the tempest is tame).
Oh grant me a house by the beach of a bay,
Where the waves can be surly in winter, and play
With the sea-weed in summer, ye bountiful powers!
And I'd leave all the hurry, the noise, and the fray,
For a house full of books, and a garden of flowers.

ENVOY.

Gods, give or withhold it! Your "yea" and your "nay"
Are immutable, heedless of outcry of ours:
But life *is* worth living, and here we would stay
For a house full of books, and a garden of flowers.

## BALLADE OF THE BOOKMAN'S PARADISE.

A. LANG. *From 'Rhymes à la Mode.' 1885.*

There *is* a Heaven, or here, or there,—
A Heaven there is, for me and you,
Where bargains meet for purses spare,
Like ours, are not so far and few.
Thuanus' bees go humming through
The learned groves, 'neath rainless skies,
O'er volumes old and volumes new,
Within that Bookman's Paradise!

There treasures bound for Longepierre
Keep brilliant their morocco blue,
There Hookes' 'Amanda' is not rare,
Nor early tracts upon Peru!
Racine is common as Rotrou,
No Shakspere Quarto search defies,
And Caxtons grow as blossoms grew,
Within that Bookman's Paradise!

There's Eve,—not our first mother fair,—
But Clovis Eve, a binder true;
Thither does Bauzonnet repair,
Derome, Le Gascon, Padeloup!
But never come the cropping crew,
That dock a volume's honest size,
Nor they that "letter" backs askew,
Within that Bookman's Paradise!

#### ENVOY.

Friend, do not Heber and De Thou,
And Scott, and Southey, kind and wise,
*La chasse au bouquin* still pursue
Within that Bookman's Paradise?

## THE ROWFANT BOOKS.

A. LANG.

*Ballade en guise de rondeau, written for the catalogue of Mr. Frederick Locker's books.*

The Rowfant books, how fair they show,
The Quarto quaint, the Aldine tall,
Print, autograph, portfolio!
Back from the outer air they call,
The athletes from the Tennis ball,
This Rhymer from his rod and hooks,—
Would I could sing them, one and all,—
The Rowfant books!

The Rowfant books! In sun and snow
They're dear, but most when tempests fall;
The folio towers above the row
As once, o'er minor prophets,—Saul!
What jolly jest books, and what small
"Dear dumpy Twelves" to fill the nooks.
You do not find on every stall
The Rowfant books!

The Rowfant books! These long ago
Were chained within some College hall;
These manuscripts retain the glow
Of many a colored capital;
While yet the satires keep their gall,
While the Pastissier puzzles cooks,
Theirs is a joy that does not pall,—
The Rowfant books!

#### ENVOY.

The Rowfant books,—ah, magical
As famed Armida's golden looks,
They hold the Rhymer for their thrall,—
The Rowfant books!

## THE ROWFANT LIBRARY.

A. LANG. *Written for the catalogue of Mr. Frederick Locker's books.*

I mind me of the Shepherd's saw,
For, when men spoke of Heaven, quoth he,
"It's everything that's bright and braw,
But *Bourhope's* good enough for me."

Among the green deep bosomed hills
That guard St. Mary's Loch it lies,
The silence of the pastures fills
That yeoman's homely paradise!

Enough for him his mountain lake,
His glen the burn goes singing through;
And *Rowfant*, when the thrushes wake,
Might well seem Paradise to you!

For all is old, and tried, and dear,
And all is fair, and all about
The brook that murmurs from the mere
Is dimpled with the rising trout.

And when the skies of shorter days
Are dark, and all the paths are mire,
How kindly o'er your *Books* the blaze
Sports from the cheerful study fire;

O'er Quartos, where our Fathers read
Entranced, the Book of Shakspere's play,
O'er all that Poe has dreamed of dread,
And all that Herrick sang of gay!

Rare First Editions, duly prized,
Among them dearest far I rate
The tome where *Walton's* hand revised
His magical receipts for bait.

Happy, who rich in toys like these
Forgets a weary nation's ills,
Who, from his study window sees
The circle of the Sussex hills!

But back to town my Muse must fly,
And taste the smoke, and list to them
Who cry the News, and seem to cry
(With each Gladstonian victory),
*Woe, woe unto Jerusalem!*[25]

## GHOSTS IN THE LIBRARY.

---

[25] During the General Election, November, 1885.

A. LANG. *From 'Longman's Magazine,' July, 1886.*

Suppose, when now the house is dumb,
When lights are out, and ashes fall,—
Suppose their ancient owners come
To claim our spoils of shop and stall,
Ah me! within the narrow hall
How strange a mob would meet and go,
What famous folk would haunt them all,
Octavo, quarto, folio!

The great Napoleon lays his hand
Upon this eagle-headed N,
That marks for his a pamphlet banned
By all but scandal-loving men,—
A libel from some nameless den
Of Frankfort—*Arnaud, à la Sphère*,
Wherein one spilt, with venal pen,
Lies o'er the loves of Molière.[26]

Another shade—he does not see
"Boney," the foeman of his race—
The great Sir Walter, this is he
With that grave homely Border face.
He claims his poem of the chase
That rang Benvoirlich's valley through;
And *this*, that doth the lineage trace
And fortunes of the bold Buccleuch;[27]

For these were his, and these he gave
To one who dwelt beside the Peel,
That murmurs with its tiny wave
To join the Tweed at Ashestiel.
Now thick as motes the shadows wheel,
And find their own, and claim a share
Of books wherein Ribou did deal,
Or Roulland sold to wise Colbert.[28]

What famous folk of old are here!
A royal duke comes down to us,
And greatly wants his Elzevir,

---

[26] 'Histoire des Intrigues Amoureuses de Molière et de celles de sa femme. (A la Sphère.) A Francfort, chez Frédéric Arnaud, MDCXCVII.' This anonymous tract has actually been attributed, among others, to Racine. The copy referred to is marked with a large N in red, with an eagle's head.

[27] 'The Lady of the Lake,' 1810.
  'The Lay of the Last Minstrel,' 1806.
  "To Mrs. Robert Laidlaw. Peel. From the Author."

[28] 'Dictys Cretensis.' Apud Lambertum Roulland. Lut. Paris. 1680. In red morocco, with the arms of Colbert.

His Pagan tutor, Lucius.[29]
And Beckford claims an amorous
Old heathen in morocco blue;[30]
And who demands Eobanus
But stately Jacques Auguste de Thou![31]

They come, the wise, the great, the true,
They jostle on the narrow stair,
The frolic Countess de Verrue,
Lamoignon, ay, and Longepierre,
The new and elder dead are there—
The lords of speech, and song, and pen,
Gambetta,[32] Schlegel,[33] and the rare
Drummond of haunted Hawthornden.[34]

Ah, and with those, a hundred more,
Whose names, whose deeds, are quite forgot:
Brave 'Smiths' and 'Thompsons' by the score,
Scrawled upon many a shabby 'lot.'
This play-book was the joy of Pott[35]–
Pott, for whom now no mortal grieves.
Our names, like his, remembered not,
Like his, shall flutter on fly-leaves!

At least in pleasant company
We bookish ghosts, perchance, may flit;
A man may turn a page, and sigh,
Seeing one's name, to think of it.
Beauty, or Poet, Sage, or Wit,
May ope our book, and muse awhile,
And fall into a dreaming fit,
As now we dream, and wake, and smile!

---

[29] 'L. Annæi Senecæ Opera Omnia.' Lug. Bat., apud Elzevirios. 1649. With book-plate of the Duke of Sussex.

[30] 'Stratonis Epigrammata.' Altenburgi, 1764. Straton bound up in one volume with Epictetus! From the Beckford library.

[31] 'Opera Helii Eobani Hessi.' Yellow morocco, with the first arms of De Thou. Include a poem addressed "Lange, *decus meum*." Quantity of penultimate "Eobanus" taken for granted, *metri gratiâ*.

[32] 'La Journée du Chrétien.' Coutances, 1831. With inscription, "Léon Gambetta. Rue St. Honoré. Janvier 1, 1848."

[33] Villoison's 'Homer.' Venice, 1788. With Tessier's ticket and Schlegel's book-plate.

[34] 'Les Essais de Michel.' Seigneur de Montaigne. "Pour François le Febvre de Lyon, 1695." With autograph of Gul. Drummond, and *cipresso e palma*.

[35] "The little old foxed Molière," once the property of William Pott, unknown to fame.

## THE BOOK BATTALION.[36]

George Parsons Lathrop.   *Written for the present collection.*

Wherever I go, there's a trusty battalion
That follows me faithfully, steady, and true;
Their force, when I falter, I safely may rally on,
Knowing their stoutness will carry me through:
Some fifteen hundred in order impartial,
So ranged that they tell what they mean by their looks.
Of all the armies the world can marshal
There are no better soldiers than well-tried books.

Dumb in their ranks on the shelves imprisoned,
They never retreat. Give the word, and they'll fire!
A few with scarlet and gold are bedizened,
But many muster in rough attire;
And some, with service and scars grown wizened,
Seem hardly the mates for their fellows in youth;
Yet they, and the troops armed only with quiz and
Light laughter, all battle alike for the truth.

Here are those who gave motive to sock and to buskin;
With critics, historians, poets galore;
A cheaply uniformed set of Ruskin,
Which Ruskin would hate from his heart's very core;
Molière ('99), an old calf-bound edition,
"*De Pierre Didot l'aîné, et de Firmin Didot.*"
Which, meek and demure, with a sort of contrition,
Is masking its gun-lights, with fun all aglow;

And Smollett and Fielding, as veterans battered—
Cloth stripped from their backs, and their sides out of joint,
Their pictures of life all naked and tattered
Being thus applied to themselves with a point;
And six or eight books that I wrote myself,
To look at which, even, I'm half afraid;
They brought me more labor and pleasure than pelf,
And are clamoring still because they're not paid.

But these raw levies remain still faithful,
Because they know that volumes old
Stand by me, although their eyes dim and wraithful
Remind me they seldom at profit were sold.
So I say, be they splendid or tatterdemalion,
If only you know what they mean by their looks,
You will never find a better battalion
Of soldiers to serve you than well-tried books.

---

[36] The poems thus marked were written or translated for the present collection.

## ON THE FLY-LEAF OF A BOOK OF OLD PLAYS.[37]

WALTER LEARNED. *Written for the present collection.*

At Cato's-Head in Russell Street
These leaves she sat a-stitching;
I fancy she was trim and neat,
Blue-eyed and quite bewitching.

Before her, in the street below,
All powder, ruffs, and laces,
There strutted idle London beaux
To ogle pretty faces;

While, filling many a Sedan chair
With hoop and monstrous feather,
In patch and powder London's fair
Went trooping past together.

Swift, Addison, and Pope, mayhap
They sauntered slowly past her,
Or printer's boy, with gown and cap
For Steele, went trotting faster.

For beau nor wit had she a look,
Nor lord nor lady minding;
She bent her head above this book,
Attentive to her binding.

And one stray thread of golden hair,
Caught on her nimble fingers,
Was stitched within this volume, where
Until to-day it lingers.

Past and forgotten, beaux and fair;
Wigs, powder, all out-dated;
A queer antique, the Sedan chair;
Pope, stiff and antiquated.

Yet as I turn these odd old plays,
This single stray lock finding,
I'm back in those forgotten days
And watch her at her binding.

## TOO MANY BOOKS.

ROBERT LEIGHTON. *From 'Reuben, and Other Poems.' 1875*

I would that we were only readers now,
And wrote no more, or in rare heats of soul
Sweated out thoughts when the o'er-burden'd brow

---

[37] The poems thus marked were written or translated for the present collection.

Was powerless to control.

Then would all future books be small and few,
And, freed of dross, the soul's refinèd gold;
So should we have a chance to read the new,
Yet not forego the old.

But as it is, Lord help us, in this flood
Of daily papers, books, and magazines!
We scramble blind as reptiles in the mud,
And know not what it means.

Is it the myriad spawn of vagrant tides,
Whose growth would overwhelm both sea and shore,
Yet often necessary loss, provides
Sufficient and no more?

Is it the broadcast sowing of the seeds,
And from the stones, the thorns and fertile soil,
Only enough to serve the world's great needs
Rewards the sower's toil?

Is it all needed for the varied mind?
Gives not the teeming press a book too much—
Not one, but in its dense neglect shall find
Some needful heart to touch?

Ah, who can say that even this blade of grass
No mission has—superfluous as it looks?
Then wherefore feel oppressed and cry, Alas,
There are too many books!

## FROM THE FLY-LEAF OF THE ROWFANT MONTAIGNE (FLORIO, 1603).[38]

FREDERICK LOCKER. *Written for the present collection.*

Of yore, when books were few and fine,
Will Shakspere cut these leaves of mine,
But when he passed I went astray
Till bought by Pope, a gift for Gay.
Then, later on, betwixt my pages
A nose was poked—the Bolt-Court Sage's.

But though the Fame began with Rawleigh,
And had not dwindled with Macaulay,
Though still I tincture many tomes
Like Lowell's pointed sense, and Holmes',
For me the halcyon days have past—
I'm here, and with a dunce at last.

---

[38] The poems thus marked were written or translated for the present collection.

## MY BOOKS.

Henry Wadsworth Longfellow.  *Written in December, 1881.*

Sadly as some old mediæval knight
Gazed at the arms he could no longer wield,
The sword two-handed and the shining shield
Suspended in the hall, and full in sight,
While secret longings for the lost delight
Of tourney or adventure in the field
Came over him, and tears but half concealed
Trembled and fell upon his beard of white,
So I behold these books upon their shelf,
My ornaments and arms of other days;
Not wholly useless, though no longer used,
For they remind me of my other self,
Younger and stronger, and the pleasant ways,
In which I walked, now clouded and confused.

## THE SOULS OF BOOKS.

Edward Bulwer, Lord Lytton.  *From 'Earlier Poems.'*

### I.

Sit here and muse!—it is an antique room—
High-roof'd, with casements, through whose purple pane
Unwilling Daylight steals amidst the gloom,
Shy as a fearful stranger.
There They reign
(In loftier pomp than waking life had known),
The Kings of Thought!—not crown'd until the grave.
When Agamemnon sinks into the tomb,
The beggar Homer mounts the Monarch's throne!
Ye ever-living and imperial Souls,
Who rule us from the page in which ye breathe,
All that divide us from the clod ye gave!—
Law—Order—Love—Intelligence—the Sense
Of Beauty—Music and the Minstrel's wreath!—
What were our wanderings if without your goals?
As air and light, the glory ye dispense
Becomes our being—who of us can tell
What he had been, had Cadmus never taught
The art that fixes into form the thought—
Had Plato never spoken from his cell,
Or his high harp blind Homer never strung?
Kinder all earth hath grown since genial Shakspere sung!

## II.

Hark! while we muse, without the walls is heard
The various murmur of the laboring crowd,
How still, within those archive-cells interr'd,
The Calm Ones reign!—and yet they rouse the loud
Passions and tumults of the circling world!
From them, how many a youthful Tully caught
The zest and ardor of the eager Bar;
From them, how many a young Ambition sought
Gay meteors glancing o'er the sands afar—
By them each restless wing has been unfurl'd,
And their ghosts urge each rival's rushing car!
They made yon Preacher zealous for the truth;
They made yon Poet wistful for the star;
Gave Age its pastime—fired the cheek of Youth—
The unseen sires of all our beings are,—

## III.

And now so still! This, Cicero, is thy heart;
I hear it beating through each purple line.
This is thyself, Anacreon—yet, thou art
Wreath'd, as in Athens, with the Cnidian vine.
I ope thy pages, Milton, and, behold,
Thy spirit meets me in the haunted ground!—
Sublime and eloquent, as while, of old,
"It flamed and sparkled in its crystal bound;"[39] These *are* your-
selves—your life of life! The Wise,
(Minstrel or Sage) *out* of their books are clay;
But *in* their books, as from their graves, they rise,
Angels—that, side by side, upon our way,
Walk with and warn us!

Hark! the world so loud,
And they, the movers of the world, so still!

What gives this beauty to the grave? the shroud
Scarce wraps the Poet, than at once there cease
Envy and Hate! "Nine cities claim him dead,
Through which the living Homer begg'd his bread!"
And what the charm that can such health distil
From wither'd leaves—oft poisons in their bloom?
We call some books immoral! *Do they live?*
If so, believe me, TIME hath made them pure.
In Books, the veriest wicked rest in peace—
God wills that nothing evil shall endure;

---

[39] 'Comus.'

The grosser parts fly off and leave the whole,
As the dust leaves the disembodied soul!
Come from thy niche, Lucretius! Thou didst give
Man the black creed of Nothing in the tomb!
Well, when we read thee, does the dogma taint?
No; with a listless eye we pass it o'er,
And linger only on the hues that paint
The Poet's spirit lovelier than his lore.
None learn from thee to cavil with their God;
None commune with thy genius to depart
Without a loftier instinct of the heart.
Thou mak'st no Atheist—thou but mak'st the mind
Richer in gifts which Atheists best confute—
FANCY AND THOUGHT! 'Tis these that from the sod
Lift us! The life which soars above the brute
Ever and mightiest, breathes from a great Poet's lute!
Lo! that grim Merriment of Hatred;[40]—born
Of him,—the Master-Mocker of Mankind,
Beside the grin of whose malignant spleen,
Voltaire's gay sarcasm seems a smile serene,—
Do we not place it in our children's hands,
Leading young Hope through Lemuel's fabled lands?—
God's and man's libel in that foul yahoo!—
Well, and what mischief can the libel do?
O impotence of Genius to belie
Its glorious task—its mission from the sky!
Swift wrote this book to wreak a ribald scorn
On aught the Man should love or Priest should mourn—
And lo! the book, from all its ends beguil'd,
A harmless wonder to some happy child!

## IV.

All books grow homilies by time; they are
Temples, at once, and Landmarks. In them, we
Who *but* for them, upon that inch of ground
We call "THE PRESENT," from the cell could see
No daylight trembling on the dungeon bar;
Turn, as we list, the globe's great axle round,
And feel the Near less household than the Far!
Traverse all space, and number every star,
There is no Past, so long as Books shall live!
A disinterr'd Pompeii wakes again
For him who seeks yon well; lost cities give
Up their untarnish'd wonders, and the reign

---

[40] 'Gulliver's Travels.'

Of Jove revives and Saturn:—at our will
Rise dome and tower on Delphi's sacred hill;
Bloom Cimon's trees in Academe;[41]—along
Leucadia's headland, sighs the Lesbian's song;
With Ægypt's Queen once more we sail the Nile,
And learn how worlds are barter'd for a smile:—
Rise up, ye walls, with gardens blooming o'er,
Ope but that page—lo, Babylon once more!

### V.

Ye make the Past our heritage and home:
And is this all? No; by each prophet-sage—
No; by the herald souls that Greece and Rome
Sent forth, like hymns, to greet the Morning Star
That rose on Bethlehem—by thy golden page,
Melodious Plato—by thy solemn dreams,
World-wearied Tully!—and, above ye all,
By THIS, the Everlasting Monument
Of God to mortals, on whose front the beams
Flash glory-breathing day—our lights ye are
To the dark Bourne beyond; in you are sent
The types of Truths whose life is THE TO-COME;
In you soars up the Adam from the fall;
In you the FUTURE as the PAST is given—
Ev'n in our death ye bid us hail our birth;—
Unfold these pages, and behold the Heaven,
Without one gravestone left upon the Earth?

## DE LIBRIS.[42]

COSMO MONKHOUSE. *Written for the present collection.*

True—there are books and books. There's Gray,
For instance, and there's Bacon;
There's Longfellow, and Monstrelet,
And also Colton's 'Lacon,'
With 'Laws of Whist' and those of Libel,
And Euclid, and the Mormon Bible.

And some are dear as friends, and some
We keep because we need them;
And some we ward from worm and thumb,
And love too well to read them.
My own are poor, and mostly new,
But I've an Elzevir or two.

---

[41] Plut. in 'Vit. Cim.'
[42] The poems thus marked were written or translated for the present collection.

That as a gift is prized, the next
For trouble in the finding;
This Aldine for its early text,
That Plantin for the binding;
This sorry Herrick hides a flower,
The record of one perfect hour.

But whether it be worth or looks
We gently love or strongly,
Such virtue doth reside in books
We scarce can love them wrongly;
To sages an eternal school,
A hobby (harmless) to the fool.

Nor altogether fool is he
Who orders, free from doubt,
Those books which "no good library
Should ever be without,"
And blandly locks the well-glazed door
On tomes that issue never more.

Less may we scorn his cases grand,
Where safely, surely linger
Fair virgin fields of type, unscanned
And innocent of finger.
There rest, preserved from dust accurst,
The first editions—and the worst.

And least of all should we that write
With easy jest deride them,
Who hope to leave when "lost to sight"
The best of us inside them,
Dear shrines! where many a scribbler's name
Has lasted—longer than his fame.

## EX LIBRIS.[43]

ARTHUR J. MUNBY. *Written for the present collection.*

Man that is born of woman finds a charm
In that which he is born of. She it is
Who moulds him with a frown or with a kiss
To good or ill, to welfare or to harm:
But, when he has attain'd her soft round arm
And drawn it through his own, and made her his,
He through her eyes beholds a wider bliss,
As sweet as that she gives him, and as warm.

What bliss? We dare not name it: her fond looks

---

[43] The poems thus marked were written or translated for the present collection.

Are jealous too; she hardly understands,
Girt by her children's laughter or their cries,
The stately smooth companionship of books:
And yet to her we owe it, to her hands
And to her heart, that books can make us wise.

## ON AN INSCRIPTION.[44]

ARTHUR J. MUNBY.

*"Edward Danenhill: Book given him by Joseph Wise, April y*$^e$* 27*$^{th}$*, 1741," was the inscription in a copy of Carew's 'Poems' (1651). Written for the present collection.*

A man unknown this volume gave,
So long since, to his unknown friend,
Ages ago, their lives had end,
And each in some obscurest grave
Lies mixt with earth: none now would care
To ask or who or what they were.
But, though these two are underground,
Their book is here, all safe and sound;
And he who wrote it (yea, and more
Than a whole hundred years before)
He, the trim courtier, old Carew,
And all the loves he feign'd or knew,
Have won from Aphrodite's eye
Some show of immortality.
'Tis ever thus; by Nature's will
The gift outlasts the giver still;
And Love itself lives not so long
As doth a lover's feeblest song.
But doubly hard is that man's case,
For whom and for his earnest rhymes
Neither his own nor after-times
Have any work, have any place:
Who through a hundred years shall find
No echoing voice, no answering mind;
And, when this tann'd and tawny page
Has one more century of age,
And others buy the book anew,
Because they care for old Carew,
Not one who reads shall care or know
What name was his, who owns it now:
But all he wrote and all he did
Shall be in such oblivion hid

---
[44] The poems thus marked were written or translated for the present collection.

As hides the blurr'd and broken stones
That cover his forgotten bones.

## TO MY BOOKS.

CAROLINE NORTON. *From the 'Dream and other Poems.' 1840.*

Silent companions of the lonely hour,
Friends, who can never alter or forsake,
Who for inconstant roving have no power,
And all neglect, perforce, must calmly take,
Let me return to YOU; this turmoil ending
Which worldly cares have in my spirit wrought,
And, o'er your old familiar pages bending,
Refresh my mind with many a tranquil thought;
Till, haply meeting there, from time to time,
Fancies, the audible echo of my own,
'T will be like hearing in a foreign clime
My native language spoke in friendly tone,
And with a sort of welcome I shall dwell
On these, my unripe musings, told so well.

## 'DESULTORY READING.'

F. M. P. *From the London 'Spectator' of January 16, 1886.*

O finest essence of delicious rest!
To bid for some short space the busy mill
Of anxious, ever-grinding thought be still;
And let the weary brain and throbbing breast
Be by another's cooling hand caressed.
This volume in my hand, I hold a charm
Which lifts me out of reach of wrong or harm.
I sail away from trouble; and most blessed
Of every blessing, can myself forget:
Can rise above the instance low and poor
Into the mighty law that governs yet.
This hingèd cover, like a well hung door,
Shuts out the noises of the jangling day,
These fair leaves fan unwelcome thoughts away.

## THE BOOKWORM.

THOMAS PARNELL. *Translated from the Latin of Theodore Beza.*

Come hither, boy, we'll hunt to-day

The bookworm, ravening beast of prey,
Produc'd by parent Earth, at odds,
As fame reports it, with the gods.
Him frantic hunger wildly drives
Against a thousand authors' lives:
Through all the fields of wit he flies;
Dreadful his head with clustering eyes,
With horns without, and tusks within,
And scales to serve him for a skin.
Observe him nearly, lest he climb
To wound the bards of ancient time,
Or down the vale of fancy go
To tear some modern wretch below.
On every corner fix thine eye,
Or ten to one he slips thee by.

See where his teeth a passage eat:
We'll rouse him from his deep retreat.
But who the shelter's forc'd to give?
'Tis sacred Virgil, as I live!
From leaf to leaf, from song to song
He draws the tadpole form along,
He mounts the gilded edge before,
He's up, he scuds the cover o'er,
He turns, he doubles, there he past,
And here we have him, caught at last.

Insatiate brute, whose teeth abuse
The sweetest servants of the Muse—
Nay, never offer to deny,
I took thee in the fact to fly.
His rose nipt in every page,
My poor Anacreon mourns thy rage;
By thee my Ovid wounded lies;
By thee my Lesbia's Sparrow dies;
Thy rabid teeth have half destroy'd
The work of love in Biddy Floyd;
They rent Belinda's locks away,
And spoil'd the Blouzelind of Gay.
For all, for every single deed,
Relentless justice bids thee bleed:
Then fall a victim to the Nine
Myself the priest, my desk the shrine.

Bring Homer, Virgil, Tasso near,
To pile a sacred altar here:
Hold, boy, thy hand outruns thy wit,
You reach'd the plays that Dennis writ;

You reach'd me Philips' rustic strain;
Pray take your mortal bards again.

Come, bind the victim,—there he lies,
And here between his numerous eyes
This venerable dust I lay
From manuscripts just swept away.
The goblet in my hand I take,
For the libation's yet to make:
A health to poets! all their days
May they have bread, as well as praise;
Sense may they seek, and less engage
In papers fill'd with party rage.
But if their riches spoil their vein,
Ye Muses, make them poor again.

Now bring the weapon, yonder blade
With which my tuneful pens are made.
I strike the scales that arm thee round,
And twice and thrice I print the wound;
The sacred altar floats with red,
And now he dies, and now he's dead.

How like the son of Jove I stand,
This Hydra stretch'd beneath the hand!
Lay bare the monster's entrails here,
And see what dangers threat the year:
Ye gods! what sonnet on a wench!
What lean translations out of French!
'Tis plain, this lobe is so unsound,
S—prints, before the months go round.

But hold, before I close the scene
The sacred altar should be clean.
O had I Shadwell's second bays,
Or, Tate, thy pert and humble lays!
(Ye pair, forgive me, when I vow
I never miss'd your works till now,)
I'd tear the leaves to wipe the shrine,
That only way you please the Nine:
But since I chance to want these two,
I'll make the songs of Durfey do.

Rent from the corps, on yonder pin,
I hang the scales that brac'd it in;
I hang my studious morning gown,
And write my own inscription down.

"This trophy from the Python won,
This robe, in which the deed was done,

These, Parnell, glorying in the feat
Hung on these shelves, the Muses seat.
Here Ignorance and Hunger found
Large realms of wit to ravage round;
Here Ignorance and Hunger fell
Two foes in one I sent to hell.
Ye poets who my labors see
Come share the triumph all with me!
Ye critics, born to vex the Muse,
Go mourn the grand ally you lose!"

## AMONG MY BOOKS.

SAMUEL MINTURN PECK. *From 'Cap and Bells.' 1886.*

Among my books—what rest is there
From wasting woes! what balm for care!
If ills appall or clouds hang low,
And drooping, dim the fleeting show,
I revel still in visions rare.
At will I breathe the classic air,
The wanderings of Ulysses share;
Or see the plume of Bayard flow
Among my books.

Whatever face the world may wear—
If Lillian has no smile to spare,
For others let her beauty blow,
Such favors I can well forego;
Perchance forget the frowning fair
Among my books.

## A RUINED LIBRARY.[45]

WALTER HERRIES POLLOCK. *Written for the present collection.*

"Imperious Cæsar dead and turn'd to clay
Might stop a hole to keep the wind away."
Here the live thought of buried Cæsar's brain
Has served a lazy slut to lay the train
That lights a dunce's fire. Here Homer's seen
All torn or crumpled in the pettish spleen
Of some spoilt urchin. Here a leaf from Glanvil
Is reft to mark a place in 'On the Anvil.'
Here, too, a heavy-blotted Shakspere's page
Holds up an inky mirror to the age;
Here looking round you're but too sure to see a

---

[45] The poems thus marked were written or translated for the present collection.

Heart-breaking wreck from the 'Via Jacobæa;'
Here some rare pamphlet, long a-missing, lurks
In an odd volume of 'Lord Bacon's Works;'
Here may you find a Stillingfleet or Blair
Usurp the binding of a lost Voltaire;
And here a tattered Boyle doth gape ungently
Upon a damp-disfigured 'Life of Bentley.'
Here half a Rabelais jostles for position
The quarter of a 'Spanish Inquisition;'
Here Young's 'Night Thoughts' lie mixed with Swinburne's 'Ballads'
'Mid scraps of works on Poisons and on Salads;
And here a rent and gilt-edged Sterne doth lack a ray
Of sun that falls upon a bulging Thackeray;
Here—but the tale's too sad at length to tell
How a book-heaven's been turned to a book-hell.

## MY BOOKS.

BRYAN WALLER PROCTER. *From 'An Autobiographical*
(BARRY CORNWALL.) *Fragment.' 1877.*

All round the room my silent servants wait,—
My friends in every season, bright and dim;
Angels and seraphim
Come down and murmur to me, sweet and low,
And spirits of the skies all come and go
Early and late;
All from the old world's divine and distant date,
From the sublimer few,
Down to the poet who but yester-eve
Sang sweet and made us grieve,
All come, assembling here in order due.
And here I dwell with Poesy, my mate,
With Erato and all her vernal sighs,
Great Clio with her victories elate,
Or pale Urania's deep and starry eyes.
O friends, whom chance and change can never harm,
Whom Death the tyrant cannot doom to die,
Within whose folding soft eternal charm
I love to lie,
And meditate upon your verse that flows,
And fertilizes whereso'er it goes,
Whether....

## TO MY BOOKS ON PARTING WITH THEM.

WILLIAM ROSCOE.

*The sale of the famous Roscoe library, made necessary by reverses in business, took place in August and September, 1816*

As one who, destined from his friends to part,
Regrets his loss, yet hopes again erewhile,
To share their converse and enjoy their smile,
And tempers as he may affliction's dart,—
Thus, loved associates! chiefs of elder Art!
Teachers of wisdom! who could once beguile
My tedious hours, and lighten every toil,
I now resign you; nor with fainting heart;
For pass a few short years, or days, or hours.
And happier seasons may their dawn unfold,
And all your sacred fellowship restore;
When, freed from earth, unlimited its powers,
Mind shall with mind direct communion hold,
And kindred spirits meet to part no more.

## AMONG MY BOOKS.

FRANCIS ST. CLAIR-ERSKINE,
EARL OF ROSSLYN.

*From 'Sonnets.' 1883.*

Alone, 'midst living works of mighty dead,
Poets and Scholars versed in history's lore,
With thoughts that reached beyond them and before,
I dream, and leave their glorious works unread;
Their greatness numbs me both in heart and head.
I cannot weep with Petrarch, and still more
I fail when I would delve the depths of yore,
And learn old Truths of modern lies instead;
The shelves frown on me blackly, with a life
That ne'er can die, and helpless to begin,
I can but own my weakness, and deplore
This waste, this barren brain, ah! once so rife
With hope and fancy. Pardon all my sin,
Great Ghosts that wander on the Eternal Shore.

## THE LIBRARY.

JOHN GODFREY SAXE.

*One of the excerpts from 'Occasional Poems' included in his 'Complete Poems'.*

Here, e'en the sturdy democrat may find,
Nor scorn their rank, the nobles of the mind;
While kings may learn, nor blush at being shown,
How Learning's patents abrogate their own.

A goodly company and fair to see;
Royal plebeians; earls of low degree;
Beggars whose wealth enriches every clime;
Princes who scarce can boast a mental dime;
Crowd here together like the quaint array
Of jostling neighbors on a market day.
Homer and Milton,—can we call them blind?—
Of godlike sight, the vision of the mind;
Shakspere, who calmly looked creation through,
"Exhausted worlds, and then imagined new;"
Plato the sage, so thoughtful and serene,
He seems a prophet by his heavenly mien;
Shrewd Socrates, whose philosophic power
Xantippe proved in many a trying hour;
And Aristophanes, whose humor run
In vain endeavor to be-"cloud" the sun;
Majestic Æschylus, whose glowing page
Holds half the grandeur of the Athenian stage;
Pindar, whose odes, replete with heavenly fire,
Proclaim the master of the Grecian lyre;
Anacreon, famed for many a luscious line
Devote to Venus and the god of wine.

I love vast libraries; yet there is a doubt
If one be better with them or without,—
Unless he use them wisely, and indeed,
Knows the high art of what and how to read,
At learning's fountain it is sweet to drink,
But 'tis a nobler privilege to think;
And oft from books apart, the thirsting mind
May make the nectar which it cannot find,
'T is well to borrow from the good and great;
'T is wise to learn; 't is godlike to create!

## IN THE LIBRARY.

CLINTON SCOLLARD. *From 'With Reed and Lyre.' 1886.*

From the oriels one by one,
Slowly fades the setting sun;
On the marge of afternoon
Stands the new-born crescent moon.
In the twilight's crimson glow
Dim the quiet alcoves grow.
Drowsy-lidded Silence smiles
On the long deserted aisles;
Out of every shadowy nook

Spirit faces seem to look.
Some with smiling eyes, and some
With a sad entreaty dumb;
He who shepherded his sheep
On the wild Sicilian steep,
He above whose grave are set
Sprays of Roman violet;
Poets, sages—all who wrought
In the crucible of thought.
Day by day as seasons glide
On the great eternal tide,
Noiselessly they gather thus
In the twilight beauteous,
Hold communion each with each,
Closer than our earthly speech,
Till within the east are born
Premonitions of the morn!

## THE BOOK-HUNTER.

FRANK DEMPSTER SHERMAN. *From the 'Century Magazine,'*
*November, 1885.*

A cup of coffee, eggs, and rolls
Sustain him on his morning strolls:
Unconscious of the passers-by,
He trudges on with downcast eye;
He wears a queer old hat and coat,
Suggestive of a style remote;
His manner is preoccupied,—
A shambling gait, from side to side.
For him the sleek, bright-windowed shop
Is all in vain,—he does not stop.
His thoughts are fixed on dusty shelves
Where musty volumes hide themselves,—
Rare prints of poetry and prose,
And quaintly lettered folios,—
Perchance a parchment manuscript,
In some forgotten corner slipped,
Or monk-illumined missal bound
In vellum with brass clasps around;
These are the pictured things that throng
His mind the while he walks along.
A dingy street, a cellar dim,
With book-lined walls, suffices him.
The dust is white upon his sleeves;
He turns the yellow, dog-eared leaves

With just the same religious look
That priests give to the Holy Book.
He does not heed the stifling air
If so he find a treasure there.
He knows rare books, like precious wines,
Are hidden where the sun ne'er shines;
For him delicious flavors dwell
In books as in old Muscatel;
He finds in features of the type
A clew to prove the grape was ripe.
And when he leaves this dismal place,
Behold, a smile lights up his face!
Upon his cheeks a genial glow, —
Within his hand Boccaccio,
A first edition worn with age,
"Firenze" on the title-page.

## THE LIBRARY.

ROBERT SOUTHEY. *Written at Keswick in 1818.*

My days among the Dead are past;
Around me I behold,
Where'er these casual eyes are cast,
The mighty minds of old;
My never-failing friends are they,
With whom I converse day by day.

With them I take delight in weal,
And seek relief in woe;
And while I understand and feel
How much to them I owe,
My cheeks have often been dedew'd
With tears of thoughtful gratitude.

My thoughts are with the Dead, with them
I live in long-past years,
Their virtues love, their faults condemn;
Partake their hopes and fears,
And from their lessons seek and find
Instruction with an humble mind.

My hopes are with the Dead, anon
My place with them shall be,
And I with them shall travel on
Through all futurity;
Yet leaving here a name, I trust,
That will not perish in the dust.

## PICTURE-BOOKS IN WINTER.

ROBERT LOUIS STEVENSON.　　　　　*From 'A Child's Garden of Verses.' 1885.*

Summer fading, winter comes—
Frosty mornings, tingling thumbs,
Window robins, winter rooks,
And the picture story-books.

Water now is turned to stone
Nurse and I can walk upon;
Still we find the flowing brooks
And the picture story-books.

All the pretty things put by,
Wait upon the children's eye
Sheep and shepherds, trees and crooks,
In the picture story-books.

We may see how all things are,
Seas and cities, near and far,
And the flying fairies' looks,
In the picture story-books.

How am I to sing your praise,
Happy chimney-corner days,
Sitting safe in nursery nooks,
Reading picture story-books?

## COMPANIONS.

A French writer (whom I love well) speaks of three kinds of companions, men, women, and books.

　　　　　　　　　　　　　　　　　　　　　　　　SIR JOHN DAVYS.

RICHARD HENRY STODDARD.　　　　　*From the 'Atlantic Monthly,' June, 1877.*

We have companions, comrade mine:
Jolly good fellows, tried and true,
Are filling their cups with the Rhenish wine,
And pledging each other, as I do you.
Never a man in all the land
But has, in his hour of need, a friend,
Who stretches to him a helping hand
And stands by him to the bitter end.
If not before, there is comfort then,
In the strong companionship of men.

But better than that, old friend of mine,
Is the love of woman, the life of life,
Whether in maiden's eyes it shine,

Or melts in the tender kiss of wife;
A heart contented to feel, not know,
That finds in the other its sole delight;
White hands that are loath to let us go,
The tenderness that is more than might!
On earth below, in heaven above,
Is there anything better than woman's love?

I do not say so, companion mine,
For what, without it, would I be here?
It lightens my troubles, like this good wine,
And, if I must weep, sheds tear for tear!
But books, old friends that are always new,
Of all good things that we know are best;
They never forsake us, as others do,
And never disturb our inward rest.
Here is truth in a world of lies,
And all that in man is great and wise!

Better than men and women, friend,
That are dust, though dear in our joy and pain,
Are the books their cunning hands have penned,
For they depart, but the books remain;
Through these they speak to us what was best
In the loving heart and the noble mind:
All their royal souls possessed
Belongs forever to all mankind!
When others fail him, the wise man looks
To the sure companionship of books.

## THE BOOK OF LIFE.

Richard Thomson.

*A Bibliographical Melody, printed in 1820 at the press of John Johnson, as a gift to the members of the Roxburghe Club.*

That Life is a Comedy oft hath been shown,
By all who Mortality's changes have known;
But more like a Volume its actions appear,
Where each Day is a Page and each Chapter a year.
'Tis a Manuscript Time shall full surely unfold,
Though with Black-Letter shaded, or shining with gold;
The Initial, like Youth, glitters bright on its Page,
But its Text is as dark—as the gloom of Old Age.
Then Life's Counsels of Wisdom engrave on thy breast,
And deep on thine Heart be her lessons imprest.

Though the Title stands first it can little declare

The Contents which the Pages ensuing shall bear;
As little the first day of Life can explain
The succeeding events which shall glide in its train,
The Book follows next, and, delighted, we trace
An Elzevir's beauty, a Guttemberg's grace;
Thus on pleasure we gaze with as raptured an eye,
Till, cut off like a Volume imperfect, we die!
Then Life's Counsels of Wisdom engrave on thy breast,
And deep on thine Heart be her lessons imprest.

Yet e'en thus imperfect, complete, or defaced,
The skill of the Printer is still to be traced;
And though death bend us early in life to his will,
The wise hand of our Author is visible still.
Like the Colophon lines is the Epitaph's lay,
Which tells of what age and what nation our day,
And, like the Device of the Printer, we bear
The form of the Founder, whose Image we wear.
Then Life's Counsels of Wisdom engrave on thy breast,
And deep on thine Heart be her lessons imprest.

The work thus completed its Boards shall inclose,
Till a Binding more bright and more beauteous it shows;
And who can deny, when Life's Vision hath past,
That the dark Boards of Death shall surround us at last.
Yet our Volume illumed with fresh splendors shall rise,
To be gazed at by Angels, and read to the skies,
Reviewed by its Author, revised by his Pen,
In a fair new Edition to flourish again.
Then Life's Counsels of Wisdom engrave on thy breast,
And deep on thine Heart be her lessons imprest.

## ON CERTAIN BOOKS.

CHARLES TENNYSON TURNER. *From 'Sonnets.' 1864.*

Faith and fixt hope these pages may peruse,
And still be faith and hope; but, O ye winds!
Blow them far off from all unstable minds,
And foolish grasping hands of youth! Ye dews
Of heaven! be pleased to rot them where they fall,
Lest loitering boys their fancies should abuse,
And they get harm by chance, that cannot choose;
So be they stain'd and sodden, each and all!
And if, perforce, on dry and gusty days,
Upon the breeze some truant leaf should rise,
Brittle with many weathers, to the skies,
Or flit and dodge about the public ways—

Man's choral shout, or organ's peal of praise
Shall shake it into dust, like older lies.

## TO HIS BOOKS.

HENRY VAUGHAN. *From 'Silex Scintillans: Sacred Poems and Pious Ejaculations.' 1678.*

Bright books: perspectives on our weak sights,
The clear projections of discerning lights,
Burning in shining thoughts, man's posthume day,
The track of fled souls in their milkie way,
The dead alive and busy, the still voice
Of enlarged spirits, kind heaven's white decoys!
Who lives with you lives like those knowing flowers
Which in commerce with light spend all their hours;
Which shut to clouds, and shadows nicely shun,
But with glad haste unveil to kiss the sun.
Beneath you all is dark and a dead night,
Which whoso lives in wants both health and sight.
By sucking you, the wise, like bees, do grow
Healing and rich, though this they do most slow,
Because most choicely; for as great a store
Have we of books as bees, of herbs, or more;
And the great task to try, then know, the good,
To discern weeds, and judge of wholesome food,
Is a rare scant performance. For man dies
Oft ere 'tis done, while the bee feeds and flies.
But you were all choice flowers; all set and drest
By old sage florists, who well knew the best;
And I amidst you all am turned to weed!
Not wanting knowledge, but for want of heed.
Then thank thyself, wild fool, that would'st not be
Content to know what was too much for thee!

## LITERATURE AND NATURE.[46]

SAMUEL WADDINGTON. *Written for the present collection.*

'Mid Cambrian heights around Dolgelly vale,
What time we scaled great Cader's rugged pile,
Or loitered idly where still meadows smile
Beside the Mawddach-stream, or far Cynfael—
Nor tome, nor rhythmic page, nor pastoral tale,
Our summer-sated senses would beguile;
Or lull our ears to melody, the while

---

[46] The poems thus marked were written or translated for the present collection.

The voiceful rill ran lilting down the dale.
In London town once more—behold, once more
The old delight returns! 'Mid heights how vast,
In Milton's verse, through what dim paths we wind;
How Keats's canvas glows, and Wordsworth's lore,
As tarn or torrent pure, by none surpass'd,
Sheds light and love—unfathomed, undefined.

## THE LIBRARY.

JOHN GREENLEAF WHITTIER. *Sung at the opening of the Library at Haverhill, Mass.*

"Let there be Light!" God spake of old,
And over chaos dark and cold,
And through the dead and formless frame
Of nature, life and order came.

Faint was the light at first that shone
On giant fern and mastodon,
On half-formed plant and beast of prey,
And man as rude and wild as they.

Age after age, like waves o'erran
The earth, uplifting brute and man;
And mind, at length, in symbols dark
Its meanings traced on stone and bark.

On leaf of palm, on sedge-wrought roll,
On plastic clay and leathern scroll,
Man wrote his thoughts; the ages passed,
And lo! the Press was found at last!

Then dead souls woke; the thoughts of men
Whose bones were dust revived again;
The cloister's silence found a tongue,
Old prophets spake, old poets sung.

And here, to-day, the dead look down,
The kings of mind again we crown;
We hear the voices lost so long,
The sage's word, the sibyl's song.

Here Greek and Roman find themselves
Alive along these crowded shelves;
And Shakspere treads again his stage,
And Chaucer paints anew his age.

As if some Pantheon's marbles broke
Their stony trance, and lived and spoke,
Life thrills along the alcoved hall,

The lords of thought awake our call.

## THE COUNTRY SQUIRE.

Tomas Yriarte. *An anonymous translation of one of the 'Literary Fables.'*

A country squire, of greater wealth than wit
(For fools are often blessed with fortune's smile),
Had built a splendid house, and furnished it
In splendid style.

"One thing is wanting," said a friend; "for, though
The rooms are fine, the furniture profuse,
You lack a library, dear sir, for show,
If not for use."

"'Tis true; but 'zounds!" replied the squire with glee,
"The lumber-room in yonder northern wing
(I wonder I ne'er thought of it) will be
The very thing.

"I'll have it fitted up without delay
With shelves and presses of the newest mode
And rarest wood, befitting every way
A squire's abode."

"And when the whole is ready, I'll dispatch
My coachman—a most knowing fellow—down
To buy me, by admeasurement, a batch
Of books in town."

But ere the library was half supplied
With all its pomps of cabinet and shelf,
The booby squire repented him, and cried
Unto himself:—

"This room is much more roomy than I thought;
Ten thousand volumes hardly would suffice
To fill it, and would cost, however bought,
A plaguy price."

"Now as I only want them for their looks,
It might, on second thoughts, be just as good,
And cost me next to nothing, if the books
Were made of wood."

"It shall be so, I'll give the shaven deal
A coat of paint—a colorable dress,
To look like calf or vellum, and conceal
Its nakedness."

"And, gilt and lettered with the author's name,
Whatever is most excellent and rare
Shall be, or seem to be ('tis all the same),
Assembled there."

The work was done; the simulated hoards
Of wit and wisdom round the chamber stood,
In binding some; and some, of course, in *boards*,
Where all were wood.

From bulky folios down to slender twelves
The choicest tomes, in many an even row
Displayed their lettered backs upon the shelves,
A goodly show.

With such a stock as seemingly surpassed
The best collection ever formed in Spain,
What wonder if the owner grew at last
Supremely vain?

What wonder, as he paced from shelf to shelf,
And conned their titles, that the squire began,
Despite his ignorance, to think himself
A learned man?

*Let every amateur, who merely looks*
*To backs and binding, take the hint, and sell*
*His costly library—for painted books*
*Would serve as well.*

## OLD BOOKS.

Anon.

*From the appendix of 'How to Read*
*a Book in the Best Way.'*
*New York, n. d.*

I must confess I love old books!
The dearest, too, perhaps most dearly;
Thick, clumpy tomes, of antique looks,
In pigskin covers fashioned queerly.

Clasped, chained, or thonged, stamped quaintly too,
With figures wondrous strange, or holy
Men and women, and cherubs, few
Might well from owls distinguish duly.

I love black-letter books that saw
The light of day at least three hundred
Long years ago; and look with awe
On works that live, so often plundered.

I love the sacred dust the more

It clings to ancient lore, enshrining
Thoughts of the dead, renowned of yore,
Embalmed in books, for age declining.

Fit solace, food, and friends more sure
To have around one, always handy,
When sinking spirits find no cure
In news, election brawls, or brandy.

In these old books, more soothing far
Than balm of Gilead or Nepenthè,
I seek an antidote for care—
Of which most men indeed have plenty.

"Five hundred times at least," I've said—
My wife assures me—"I would never
Buy more old books;" yet lists are made,
And shelves are lumbered more than ever.

Ah! that our wives could only see
How well the money is invested
In these old books, which seem to be
By them, alas! so much detested.

There's nothing hath enduring youth,
Eternal newness, strength unfailing,
Except old books, old friends, old truth,
That's ever battling—still prevailing.

'T is better in the past to live
Than grovel in the present vilely,
In clubs, and cliques, where placemen hive,
And faction hums, and dolts rank highly.

To be enlightened, counselled, led,
By master minds of former ages,
Come to old books—consult the dead—
Commune with silent saints and sages.

Leave me, ye gods! to my old books—
Polemics yield to sects that wrangle—
Vile "parish politics" to folks
Who love to squabble, scheme, and jangle.

Dearly beloved old pigskin tomes!
Of dingy hue—old bookish darlings!
Oh, cluster ever round my rooms,
And banish strifes, disputes, and snarlings.

# APPENDIX
## THE LIBRARY
## BY GEORGE CRABBE

### THE LIBRARY.

GEORGE CRABBE.

*In want and danger, the unknown poet sent this poem to Edmund Burke, who saw its merit, befriended its author, and procured its publication.*

When the sad soul, by care and grief oppressed,
Looks round the world, but looks in vain for rest,
When every object that appears in view
Partakes her gloom and seems dejected too;
Where shall affliction from itself retire?
Where fade away and placidly expire?
Alas! we fly to silent scenes in vain;
Care blasts the honors of the flowery plain;
Care veils in clouds the sun's meridian beam,
Sighs through the grove, and murmurs in the stream;
For when the soul is laboring in despair,
In vain the body breathes a purer air:
No storm-tost sailor sighs for slumbering seas—
He dreads the tempest, but invokes the breeze;
On the smooth mirror of the deep resides
Reflected woe, and o'er unruffled tides
The ghost of every former danger glides.
Thus, in the calms of life, we only see
A steadier image of our misery;
But lively gales and gently clouded skies
Disperse the sad reflections as they rise;
And busy thoughts and little cares avail
To ease the mind, when rest and reason fail.
When the dull thought, by no designs employed,
Dwells on the past, or suffered or enjoyed,
We bleed anew in every former grief,
And joys departed furnish no relief.

Not Hope herself, with all her flattering art,
Can cure this stubborn sickness of the heart:
The soul disdains each comfort she prepares,
And anxious searches for congenial cares;
Those lenient cares, which, with our own combined,
By mixed sensations ease th' afflicted mind,
And steal our grief away, and leave their own behind;
A lighter grief! which feeling hearts endure
Without regret, nor e'en demand a cure.
But what strange art, what magic can dispose
The troubled mind to change its native woes?
Or lead us, willing from ourselves, to see
Others more wretched, more undone than we?
This Books can do;—nor this alone; they give
New views to life, and teach us how to live;
They soothe the grieved, the stubborn they chastise,
Fools they admonish and confirm the wise:
Their aid they yield to all: they never shun
The man of sorrow, nor the wretch undone:
Unlike the hard, the selfish, and the proud,
They fly not sullen from the suppliant crowd;
Nor tell to various people various things,
But show to subjects what they show to kings.
Come, Child of Care! to make thy soul serene,
Approach the treasures of this tranquil scene;
Survey the dome, and, as the doors unfold,
The soul's best cure, in all her cares behold!
Where mental wealth the poor in thought may find,
And mental physic the diseased in mind;
See here the balms that passion's wounds assuage;
See coolers here, that damp the fire of rage;
Here alteratives, by slow degrees control
The chronic habits of the sickly soul;
And round the heart, and o'er the aching head,
Mild opiates here their sober influence shed.
Now bid thy soul man's busy scenes exclude,
And view composed this silent multitude:—
Silent they are—but though deprived of sound,
Here all the living languages abound;
Here all that live no more; preserved they lie,
In tombs that open to the curious eye.
Blest be the gracious Power, who taught mankind
To stamp a lasting image of the mind!
Beasts may convey, and tuneful birds may sing,
Their mutual feelings, in the opening spring;
But Man alone has skill and power to send

The heart's warm dictates to the distant friend;
'Tis his alone to please, instruct, advise
Ages remote, and nations yet to rise.
In sweet repose, when Labor's children sleep,
When Joy forgets to smile and Care to weep,
When Passion slumbers in the lover's breast,
And Fear and Guilt partake the balm of rest,
Why then denies the studious man to share
Man's common good, who feels his common care?
Because the hope is his that bids him fly
Night's soft repose, and sleep's mild power defy,
That after-ages may repeat his praise,
And fame's fair meed be his, for length of days.
Delightful prospect! when we leave behind
A worthy offspring of the fruitful mind!
Which, born and nursed through many an anxious day,
Shall all our labor, all our care repay.
Yet all are not these births of noble kind,
Not all the children of a vigorous mind;
But where the wisest should alone preside,
The weak would rule us, and the blind would guide;
Nay, man's best efforts taste of man, and show
The poor and troubled source from which they flow;
Where most he triumphs we his wants perceive,
And for his weakness in his wisdom grieve.
But though imperfect all; yet wisdom loves
This seat serene, and virtue's self approves:—
Here come the grieved, a change of thought to find;
The curious here to feed a craving mind;
Here the devout their peaceful temple choose;
And here the poet meets his favoring Muse.
With awe, around these silent walks I tread;
These are the lasting mansions of the dead:—
"The dead!" methinks a thousand tongues reply;
"These are the tombs of such as cannot die!
Crowned with eternal fame, they sit sublime,
And laugh at all the little strife of time.
Hail, then, immortals! ye who shine above,
Each, in his sphere, the literary Jove;
And ye, the common people of these skies,
A humbler crowd of nameless deities;
Whether 't is yours to lead the willing mind
Through History's mazes, and the turnings find;
Or, whether led by Science, ye retire,
Lost and bewildered in the vast desire,
Whether the Muse invites you to her bowers,

And crowns your placid brows with living flowers!
Or godlike Wisdom teaches you to show
The noblest road to happiness below;
Or men and manners prompt the easy page
To mark the flying follies of the age;
Whatever good ye boast, that good impart;
Inform the head and rectify the heart.
Lo, all in silence, all in order stand,
And mighty folios, first a lordly band;
Then quartos their well-ordered ranks maintain,
And light octavos fill a spacious plain:
See yonder, ranged in more frequented rows,
A humbler band of duodecimos;
While undistinguish'd trifles swell the scene,
The last new play and frittered magazine.
Thus 't is in life, where first the proud, the great,
In leagued assembly keep their cumbrous state:
Heavy and huge, they fill the world with dread,
Are much admired, and are but little read:
The commons next, a middle rank, are found;
Professions fruitful pour their offspring round;
Reasoners and wits are next their place allowed,
And last, of vulgar tribes a countless crowd.
First, let us view the form, the size, the dress:
For these the manners, nay the mind, express:
That weight of wood, with leathern coat o'erlaid;
Those ample clasps of solid metal made;
The close-pressed leaves, unclosed for many an age;
The dull red edging of the well-filled page;
On the broad back the stubborn ridges rolled,
Where yet the title stands in tarnished gold;
These all a sage and labored work proclaim,
A painful candidate for lasting fame:
No idle wit, no trifling verse can lurk
In the deep bosom of that weighty work;
No playful thoughts degrade the solemn style,
Nor one light sentence claims a transient smile.
Hence, in these times, untouched the pages lie,
And slumber out their immortality:
They *had* their day, when, after all his toil,
His morning study, and his midnight oil,
At length an author's ONE great work appeared,
By patient hope, and length of days endeared:
Expecting nations haled it from the press;
Poetic friends prefixed each kind address;
Princes and kings received the pond'rous gift,

And ladies read the work they could not lift.
Fashion, though Folly's child, and guide of fools,
Rules e'en the wisest, and in learning rules;
From crowds and courts to Wisdom's seat she goes,
And reigns triumphant o'er her mother's foes.
For lo! these favorites of the ancient mode
Lie all neglected like the Birthday Ode.
Ah! needless now this weight of massy chain,
Safe in themselves, the once-loved works remain;
No readers now invade their still retreat,
None try to steal them from their parent seat;
Like ancient beauties, they may now discard
Chains, bolts, and locks, and lie without a guard.
Our patient fathers trifling themes laid by,
And rolled, o'er labored works, th' attentive eye:
Page after page the much enduring men
Explored the deeps and shallows of the pen:
Till, every former note and comment known,
They marked the spacious margin with their own;
Minute corrections proved their studious care;
The little index, pointing, told us where;
And many an emendation showed the age
Looked far beyond the rubric title-page.
Our nicer palates lighter labors seek,
Cloyed with a folio-*Number* once a week;
Bibles, with cuts and comments, thus go down:
E'en light Voltaire is *numbered* through the town:
Thus physic flies abroad, and thus the law,
From men of study, and from men of straw;
Abstracts, abridgments, please the fickle times,
Pamphlets and plays, and politics and rhymes:
But though to write be now a task of ease,
The task is hard by manly arts to please,
When all our weakness is exposed to view,
And half our judges are our rivals too.
Amid these works, on which the eager eye
Delights to fix, or glides reluctant by,
When all combined, their decent pomp display,
Where shall we first our early offering pay?—
To thee, DIVINITY! to thee, the light
And guide of mortals, through their mental night;
By whom we learn our hopes and fears to guide;
To bear with pain, and to contend with pride;
When grieved, to pray; when injured, to forgive;
And with the world in charity to live.
Not truths like these inspired that numerous race,

Whose pious labors fill this ample space;
But questions nice, where doubt on doubt arose,
Awaked to war the long-contending foes.
For dubious meanings, learned polemics strove,
And wars on faith prevented works of love;
The brands of discord far around were hurled,
And holy wrath inflamed a sinful world:—
Dull though impatient, peevish though devout,
With wit, disgusting and despised without;
Saints in design, in execution men,
Peace in their looks, and vengeance in their pen.
Methinks I see, and sicken at the sight,
Spirits of spleen from yonder pile alight;
Spirits who prompted every damning page,
With pontiff pride, and still increasing rage:
Lo! how they stretch their gloomy wings around,
And lash with furious strokes the trembling ground!
They pray, they fight, they murder, and they weep,
Wolves in their vengeance, in their manners sheep;
Too well they act the prophet's fatal part,
Denouncing evil with a zealous heart;
And each, like Jonah, is displeased if God
Repent his anger, or withold his rod.
But here the dormant fury rests unsought,
And Zeal sleeps soundly by the foes she fought;
Here all the rage of controversy ends,
And rival zealots rest like bosom friends:
An Athanasian here, in deep repose,
Sleeps with the fiercest of his Arian foes;
Socinians here with Calvinists abide,
And thin partitions angry chiefs divide;
Here wily Jesuits simple Quakers meet,
And Bellarmine has rest at Luther's feet.
Great authors, for the church's glory fired,
Are for the church's peace to rest retired;
And close beside, a mystic, maudlin race,
Lie "Crumbs of Comfort for the Babes of Grace."
Against her foes Religion well defends
Her sacred truths, but often fears her friends;
If learned, their pride, if weak, their zeal she dreads,
And their hearts' weakness, who have soundest heads.
But most she fears the controversial pen,
The holy strife of disputatious men;
Who the blest Gospel's peaceful page explore,
Only to fight against its precepts more.
Near to these seats behold yon slender frames,

All closely filled and marked with modern names;
Where no fair science ever shows her face,
Few sparks of genius, and no spark of grace;
There sceptics rest, a still increasing throng,
And stretch their widening wings ten thousand strong;
Some in close fight their dubious claims maintain;
Some skirmish lightly, fly, and fight again;
Coldly profane, and impiously gay,
Their end the same, though various in their way.
When first Religion came to bless the land,
Her friends were then a firm believing band;
To doubt was then to plunge in guilt extreme,
And all was gospel that a monk could dream;
Insulted Reason fled the grov'lling soul,
For Fear to guide and visions to control:
But now, when Reason has assumed her throne,
She, in her turn demands to reign alone;
Rejecting all that lies beyond her view,
And, being judge, will be a witness too:
Insulted Faith then leaves the doubtful mind,
To seek for truth, without a power to find:
Ah! when will both in friendly beams unite,
And pour on erring man resistless light!
Next to the seats, well stored with works divine,
An ample space, PHILOSOPHY! is thine;
Our reason's guide, by whose assisting light
We trace the moral bounds of wrong and right;
Our guide through nature, from the sterile clay,
To the bright orbs of yon celestial way!
'T is thine, the great, the golden chain to trace,
Which runs through all, connecting race with race
Save where those puzzling, stubborn links remain,
Which thy inferior light pursues in vain:—
How vice and virtue in the soul contend;
How widely differ, yet how nearly blend;
What various passions war on either part,
And now confirm, now melt the yielding heart:
How Fancy loves around the world to stray,
While Judgment slowly picks his sober way;
The stores of memory and the flights sublime
Of genius, bound by neither space nor time;—
All these divine Philosophy explores,
Till, lost in awe, she wonders and adores.
From these, descending to the earth, she turns,
And matter, in its various forms, discerns;
She parts the beamy light with skill profound,

Metes the thin air, and weighs the flying sound;
'T is hers the lightning from the clouds to call,
And teach the fiery mischief where to fall.
Yet more her volumes teach—on these we look
Abstracts drawn from Nature's larger book;
Here, first described, the torpid earth appears,
And next, the vegetable robe it wears;
Where flowery tribes in valleys, fields, and groves,
Nurse the still flame, and feed the silent loves;
Loves where no grief, nor joy, nor bliss, nor pain,
Warm the glad heart or vex the laboring brain;
But as the green blood moves along the blade,
The bed of Flora on the branch is made;
Where, without passion, love instinctive lives,
And gives new life, unconscious that it gives.
Advancing still in Nature's maze, we trace,
In dens and burning plains, her savage race
With those tame tribes who on their lord attend,
And find in man a master and a friend;
Man crowns the scene, a world of wonders new,
A moral world, that well demands our view.
This world is here; for, of more lofty kind,
These neighboring volumes reason on the mind;
They paint the state of man ere yet endued
With knowledge;—man, poor, ignorant, and rude;
Then, as his state improves, their pages swell,
And all its cares, and all its comforts tell:
Here we behold how inexperience buys,
At little price, the wisdom of the wise;
Without the troubles of an active state,
Without the cares and dangers of the great,
Without the miseries of the poor, we know
What wisdom, wealth, and poverty bestow;
We see how reason calms the raging mind,
And how contending passions urge mankind:
Some, won by virtue, glow with sacred fire;
Some, lured by vice, indulge the low desire;
Whilst others, won by either, now pursue
The guilty chase, now keep the good in view;
Forever wretched, with themselves at strife,
They lead a puzzled, vexed, uncertain life;
For transient vice bequeaths a lingering pain,
Which transient virtue seeks to cure in vain.
Whilst thus engaged, high views enlarge the soul,
New interest draws, new principles control:
Nor thus the soul alone resigns her grief,

But here the tortured body finds relief;
For see where yonder sage Arachnè shapes
Her subtle gin, that not a fly escapes!
There PHYSIC fills the space, and far around,
Pile above pile her learned works abound:
Glorious their aim—to ease the laboring heart;
To war with death, and stop his flying dart;
To trace the source whence the fierce contest grew;
And life's short lease on easier terms renew;
To calm the frenzy of the burning brain;
To heal the tortures of imploring pain;
Or, when more powerful ills all efforts brave,
To ease the victim no device can save,
And smooth the stormy passage to the grave.
But man, who knows no good unmixed and pure,
Oft finds a poison where he sought a cure;
For grave deceivers lodge their labors here,
And cloud the science they pretend to clear;
Scourges for sin, the solemn tribe are sent;
Like fire and storms, they call us to repent;
But storms subside, and fires forget to rage.
*These* are eternal scourges of the age:
'T is not enough that each terrific hand
Spreads desolation round a guilty land;
But trained to ill, and hardened by its crimes,
Their pen relentless kills through future times,
Say, ye, who search these records of the dead—
Who read huge works, to boast what ye have read,
Can all the real knowledge ye possess,
Or those—if such there are—who more than guess,
Atone for each impostor's wild mistakes,
And mend the blunders pride or folly makes?
What thought so wild, what airy dream so light,
That will not prompt a theorist to write?
What art so prevalent, what proofs so strong,
That will convince him his attempt is wrong?
One in the solids finds each lurking ill,
Nor grants the passive fluids power to kill;
A learned friend some subtler reason brings,
Absolves the channels, but condemns their spring;
The subtile nerves, that shun the doctor's eye,
Escape no more his subtler theory;
The vital heat, that warms the laboring heart,
Lends a fair system to these sons of art;
The vital air, a pure and subtile stream,
Serves a foundation for an airy scheme,

Assists the doctor and supports his dream.
Some have their favorite ills, and each disease
Is but a younger branch that kills from these;
One to the gout contracts all human pain;
He views it raging in the frantic brain;
Finds it in fevers all his efforts mar,
And sees it lurking in the cold catarrh;
Bilious by some, by others nervous seen,
Rage the fantastic demons of the spleen;
And every symptom of the strange disease
With every system of the sage agrees.
Ye frigid tribe, on whom I wasted long
The tedious hours, and ne'er indulged in song;
Ye first seducers of my easy heart,
Who promised knowledge ye could not impart;
Ye dull deluders, truth's destructive foes;
Ye sons of fiction, clad in stupid prose;
Ye treacherous leaders, who, yourselves in doubt,
Light up false fires, and send us far about;—
Still may yon spider round your pages spin,
Subtile and slow, her emblematic gin!
Buried in dust and lost in silence, dwell,
Most potent, grave, and reverend friends—farewell!
Near these, and where the setting sun displays,
Through the dim window, his departing rays,
And gilds yon columns, there, on either side,
The huge Abridgments of the LAW abide;
Fruitful as vice, the dread correctors stand,
And spread their guardian terrors round the land;
Yet, as the best that human care can do
Is mixed with error, oft with evil too,
Skilled in deceit, and practised to evade,
Knaves stand secure, for whom these laws were made,
And justice vainly each expedient tries,
While art eludes it, or while power defies.
"Ah! happy age," the youthful poet sings,
"When the free nations knew not laws nor kings,
When all were blest to share a common store,
And none were proud of wealth, for none were poor,
No wars nor tumults vexed each still domain,
No thirst of empire, no desire of gain;
No proud great man, nor one who would be great,
Drove modest merit from its proper state;
Nor into distant climes would Avarice roam,
To fetch delights for Luxury at home:
Bound by no ties which kept the soul in awe,

They dwelt at liberty, and love was law!"
"Mistaken youth! each nation first was rude,
Each man a cheerless son of solitude,
To whom no joys of social life were known,
None felt a care that was not all his own;
Or in some languid clime his abject soul
Bowed to a little tyrant's stern control;
A slave, with slaves his monarch's throne he raised,
And in rude song his ruder idol praised;
The meaner cares of life were all he knew;
Bounded his pleasures, and his wishes few;
But when by slow degrees the Arts arose,
And Science wakened from her long repose;
When Commerce, rising from the bed of ease,
Ran round the land, and pointed to the seas;
When Emulation, born with jealous eye,
And Avarice, lent their spurs to industry;
Then one by one the numerous laws were made,
Those to control, and these to succor trade;
To curb the insolence of rude command,
To snatch the victim from the usurer's hand;
To awe the bold, to yield the wronged redress,
And feed the poor with Luxury's excess."
Like some vast flood, unbounded, fierce, and strong,
His nature leads ungoverned man along;
Like mighty bulwarks made to stem that tide,
The laws are formed and placed on every side;
Whene'er it breaks the bounds by these decreed,
New statutes rise, and stronger laws succeed;
More and more gentle grows the dying stream,
More and more strong the rising bulwarks seem;
Till, like a miner working sure and slow,
Luxury creeps on, and ruins all below;
The basis sinks, the ample piles decay;
The stately fabric shakes and falls away;
Primeval want and ignorance come on,
But Freedom, that exalts the savage state, is gone.
Next HISTORY ranks;—there full in front she lies,
And every nation her dread tale supplies;
Yet History has her doubts, and every age
With sceptic queries marks the passing page;
Records of old nor later date are clear,
Too distant those, and these are placed too near;
There time conceals the objects from our view,
Here our own passions and a writer's too:
Yet, in these volumes, see how states arose!

Guarded by virtue from surrounding foes;
Their virtue lost, and of their triumphs vain,
Lo! how they sunk to slavery again!
Satiate with power, of fame and wealth possessed,
A nation grows too glorious to be blest;
Conspicuous made, she stands the mark of all,
And foes join foes to triumph in her fall.
Thus speaks the page that paints ambition's race,
The monarch's pride, his glory, his disgrace;
The headlong course that maddening heroes run,
How soon triumphant, and how soon undone;
How slaves, turned tyrants, offer crowns to sale,
And each fallen nation's melancholy tale.
Lo! where of late the Book of Martyrs stood,
Old pious tracts, and Bibles bound in wood;
There, such the taste of our degenerate age,
Stand the profane delusions of the STAGE:
Yet virtue owns the TRAGIC MUSE a friend,
Fable her means, morality her end;
For this she rules all passions in their turns,
And now the bosom bleeds, and now it burns;
Pity with weeping eye surveys her bowl,
Her anger swells, her terror chills the soul;
She makes the vile to virtue yield applause,
And own her sceptre while they break her laws;
For vice in others is abhorred of all,
And villains triumph when the worthless fall.
Not thus her sister COMEDY prevails,
Who shoots at Folly, for her arrow fails;
Folly, by Dulness armed, eludes the wound,
And harmless sees the feathered shafts rebound;
Unhurt she stands, applauds the archer's skill,
Laughs at her malice, and is Folly still.
Yet well the Muse portrays, in fancied scenes,
What pride will stoop to, what profession means;
How formal fools the farce of state applaud;
How caution watches at the lips of fraud;
The wordy variance of domestic life;
The tyrant husband, the retorting wife;
The snares for innocence, the lie of trade,
And the smooth tongue's habitual masquerade.
With her the Virtues to obtain a place,
Each gentle passion, each becoming grace;
The social joy in life's securer road,
Its easy pleasure, its substantial good;
The happy thought that conscious virtue gives,

# APPENDIX 73

And all that ought to live, and all that lives.
But who are these? Methinks a noble mien
And awful grandeur in their form are seen,
Now in disgrace· what though by time is spread
Polluting dust o'er every reverend head;
What though beneath yon gilded tribe they lie,
And dull observers pass insulting by:
Forbid it shame, forbid it decent awe,
What seems so grave, should no attention draw!
Come, let us then with reverend step advance,
And greet—the ancient worthies of ROMANCE.
Hence, ye profane! I feel a former dread,
A thousand visions float around my head:
Hark! hollow blasts through empty courts resound,
And shadowy forms with staring eyes stalk round;
See! moats and bridges, walls and castles rise,
Ghosts, fairies, demons, dance before our eyes;
Lo! magic verse inscribed on golden gate;
And bloody hand that beckons on to fate:—
"And who art thou, thou little page, unfold?
Say, doth thy lord my Claribel withhold?
Go tell him straight, Sir Knight, thou must resign
The captive queen;—for Claribel is mine."
Away he flies; and now for bloody deeds,
Black suits of armor, masks, and foaming steeds;
The giant falls; his recreant throat I seize,
And from his corselet take the massy keys:—
Dukes, lords, and knights in long procession move,
Released from bondage with my virgin love:—
She comes! she comes! in all the charms of youth,
Unequalled love, and unsuspected truth!
Ah! happy he who thus, in magic themes,
O'er worlds bewitched, in early rapture dreams,
Where wild Enchantment waves her potent wand,
And Fancy's beauties fill her fairy land;
Where doubtful objects strange desires excite,
And Fear and Ignorance afford delight.
But lost, for ever lost, to me these joys,
Which Reason scatters, and which Time destroys;
Too dearly bought: maturer judgment calls
My busied mind from tales and madrigals;
My doughty giants all are slain or fled
And all my knights—blue, green, and yellow—dead!
No more the midnight fairy tribe I view,
All in the merry moonshine tippling dew;
E'en the last lingering fiction of the brain,

The churchyard ghost is now at rest again;
And all these wayward wanderings of my youth
Fly Reason's power, and shun the light of Truth.
With Fiction then does real joy reside,
And is our reason the delusive guide?
Is it then right to dream the sirens sing?
Or mount enraptured on the dragon's wing?
No; 't is the infant mind, to care unknown,
That makes th' imagined paradise its own;
Soon as reflections in the bosom rise,
Light slumbers vanish from the clouded eyes:
The tear and smile, that once together rose,
Are then divorced; the head and heart are foes:
Enchantment bows to Wisdom's serious plan,
And Pain and Prudence make and mar the man.
While thus, of power and fancied empire vain,
With various thoughts my mind I entertain;
While books, my slaves, with tyrant hand I seize,
Pleased with the pride that will not let them please,
Sudden I find terrific thoughts arise,
And sympathetic sorrow fills my eyes;
For, lo! while yet my heart admits the wound,
I see the CRITIC army ranged around.
Foes to our race! if ever ye have known
A father's fears for offspring of your own;
If ever, smiling o'er a lucky line,
Ye thought the sudden sentiment divine,
Then paused and doubted, and then, tired of doubt,
With rage as sudden dashed the stanza out;—
If, after fearing much and pausing long,
Ye ventured on the world your labored song,
And from the crusty critics of those days
Implored the feeble tribute of their praise;
Remember now the fears that moved you then,
And, spite of truth, let mercy guide your pen.
What vent'rous race are ours! what mighty foes
Lie waiting all around them to oppose!
What treacherous friends betray them to the fight!
What dangers threaten them:—yet still they write:
A hapless tribe! to every evil born,
Whom villains hate, and fools affect to scorn:
Strangers they come, amid a world of woe,
And taste the largest portion ere they go.
Pensive I spoke, and cast mine eyes around;
The roof, methought, returned a solemn sound;
Each column seemed to shake, and clouds, like smoke,

From dusty piles and ancient volumes broke;
Gathering above, like mists condensed they seem,
Exhaled in summer from the rushy stream;
Like flowing robes they now appear, and twine
Round the large members of a form divine;
His silver beard, that swept his aged breast,
His piercing eye, that inward light expressed,
Were seen—but clouds and darkness veiled the rest.
Fear chilled my heart: to one of mortal race,
How awful seemed the Genius of the place!
So in Cimmerian shores, Ulysses saw
His parent-shade, and shrunk in pious awe;
Like him I stood, and wrapped in thought profound,
When from the pitying power broke forth a solemn sound:—
"Care lives with all; no rules, no precepts save
The wise from woe, no fortitude the brave;
Grief is to man as certain as the grave:
Tempests and storms in life's whole progress rise,
And hope shines dimly through o'erclouded skies.
Some drops of comfort on the favored fall,
But showers of sorrow are the lot of *all*:
Partial to talents, then, shall Heaven withdraw
Th' afflicting rod, or break the general law?
Shall he who soars, inspired by loftier views,
Life's little cares and little pains refuse?
Shall he not rather feel a double share
Of mortal woe, when doubly armed to bear?
"Hard is his fate who builds his peace of mind
On the precarious mercy of mankind;
Who hopes for wild and visionary things,
And mounts o'er unknown seas with vent'rous wings;
But as, of various evils that befall
The human race, some portion goes to all;
To him perhaps the milder lot's assigned
Who feels his consolation in his mind.
And, locked within his bosom, bears about
A mental charm for every care without.
E'en in the pangs of each domestic grief,
Or health or vigorous hope affords relief;
And every wound the tortured bosom feels,
Or virtue bears, or some preserver heals;
Some generous friend of ample power possessed;
Some feeling heart, that bleeds for the distressed;
Some breast that glows with virtues all divine;
Some noble RUTLAND, misery's friend and thine.
"Nor say, the Muse's song, the Poet's pen,

Merit the scorn they meet from little men.
With cautious freedom if the numbers flow,
Not wildly high, nor pitifully low;
If vice alone their honest aims oppose,
Why so ashamed their friends, so loud their foes?
Happy for men in every age and clime,
If all the sons of vision dealt in rhyme.
Go on, then, Son of Vision! still pursue
Thy airy dreams; the world is dreaming too.
Ambition's lofty views, the pomp of state,
The pride of wealth, the splendor of the great,
Stripped of their mask, their cares and troubles known,
Are visions far less happy than thy own:
Go on! and, while the sons of care complain,
Be wisely gay and innocently vain;
While serious souls are by their fears undone,
Blow sportive bladders in the beamy sun,
And call them worlds! and bid the greatest show
More radiant colors in their worlds below:
Then, as they break, the slaves of care reprove,
And tell them, Such are all the toys they love.

# A FINAL WORD.
## THE COLLECTOR TO HIS LIBRARY.[47]

*Brown Books of mine, who never yet*
*Have caused me anguish or regret,—*
*Save when some fiend in human shape*
*Has set your tender sides agape,*
*Or soiled with some unmanly smear*
*The whiteness of your page sincere,*
*Or scored you with some phrase inane,*
*The bantling of his idle brain,—*
*I love you: and because must end*
*This commerce between friend and friend,*
*I do beseech each kindly fate—*
*To each and all I supplicate—*
*That you whom I have loved so long*
*May not be vended "for a song,"—*
*That you, my dear desire and care,*
*May 'scape the common thoroughfare,*
*The dust, the eating rain, and all*
*The shame and squalor of the stall.*
*Rather I trust your lot may touch*
*Some Crœsus—if there should be such—*
*To buy you, and that you may so*
*From Crœsus unto Crœsus go*
*Till that inevitable day*
*When comes your moment of decay.*

*This, more than other good, I pray.*

Austin Dobson.

---

[47] The poems thus marked were written or translated for the present collection.

Lector House believes that a society develops through a two-fold approach of continuous learning and adaptation, which is derived from the study of classic literary works spread across the historic timeline of literature records. Therefore, we aim at reviving, repairing and redeveloping all those inaccessible or damaged but historically as well as culturally important literature across subjects so that the future generations may have an opportunity to study and learn from past works to embark upon a journey of creating a better future.

This book is a result of an effort made by Lector House towards making a contribution to the preservation and repair of original ancient works which might hold historical significance to the approach of continuous learning across subjects.

**HAPPY READING & LEARNING!**

LECTOR HOUSE LLP
E-MAIL: lectorpublishing@gmail.com

Lightning Source UK Ltd.
Milton Keynes UK
UKHW010648090820
367908UK00002B/355